C-4958   CAREER EXAMINATION SERIES

This is your
PASSBOOK for...

Homeless Services Representative III

Test Preparation Study Guide
Questions & Answers

COPYRIGHT NOTICE

This book is SOLELY intended for, is sold ONLY to, and its use is RESTRICTED to individual, bona fide applicants or candidates who qualify by virtue of having seriously filed applications for appropriate license, certificate, professional and/or promotional advancement, higher school matriculation, scholarship, or other legitimate requirements of education and/or governmental authorities.

This book is NOT intended for use, class instruction, tutoring, training, duplication, copying, reprinting, excerption, or adaptation, etc., by:

1) Other publishers
2) Proprietors and/or Instructors of "Coaching" and/or Preparatory Courses
3) Personnel and/or Training Divisions of commercial, industrial, and governmental organizations
4) Schools, colleges, or universities and/or their departments and staffs, including teachers and other personnel
5) Testing Agencies or Bureaus
6) Study groups which seek by the purchase of a single volume to copy and/or duplicate and/or adapt this material for use by the group as a whole without having purchased individual volumes for each of the members of the group
7) Et al.

Such persons would be in violation of appropriate Federal and State statutes.

PROVISION OF LICENSING AGREEMENTS – Recognized educational, commercial, industrial, and governmental institutions and organizations, and others legitimately engaged in educational pursuits, including training, testing, and measurement activities, may address request for a licensing agreement to the copyright owners, who will determine whether, and under what conditions, including fees and charges, the materials in this book may be used them. In other words, a licensing facility exists for the legitimate use of the material in this book on other than an individual basis. However, it is asseverated and affirmed here that the material in this book CANNOT be used without the receipt of the express permission of such a licensing agreement from the Publishers. Inquiries re licensing should be addressed to the company, attention rights and permissions department.

All rights reserved, including the right of reproduction in whole or in part, in any form or by any means, electronic or mechanical, including photocopying, recording, or by any information storage and retrieval system, without permission in writing from the Publisher.

Copyright © 2025 by
National Learning Corporation

212 Michael Drive, Syosset, NY 11791
(516) 921-8888 • www.passbooks.com
E-mail: info@passbooks.com

PASSBOOK® SERIES

THE *PASSBOOK® SERIES* has been created to prepare applicants and candidates for the ultimate academic battlefield – the examination room.

At some time in our lives, each and every one of us may be required to take an examination – for validation, matriculation, admission, qualification, registration, certification, or licensure.

Based on the assumption that every applicant or candidate has met the basic formal educational standards, has taken the required number of courses, and read the necessary texts, the *PASSBOOK® SERIES* furnishes the one special preparation which may assure passing with confidence, instead of failing with insecurity. Examination questions – together with answers – are furnished as the basic vehicle for study so that the mysteries of the examination and its compounding difficulties may be eliminated or diminished by a sure method.

This book is meant to help you pass your examination provided that you qualify and are serious in your objective.

The entire field is reviewed through the huge store of content information which is succinctly presented through a provocative and challenging approach – the question-and-answer method.

A climate of success is established by furnishing the correct answers at the end of each test.

You soon learn to recognize types of questions, forms of questions, and patterns of questioning. You may even begin to anticipate expected outcomes.

You perceive that many questions are repeated or adapted so that you can gain acute insights, which may enable you to score many sure points.

You learn how to confront new questions, or types of questions, and to attack them confidently and work out the correct answers.

You note objectives and emphases, and recognize pitfalls and dangers, so that you may make positive educational adjustments.

Moreover, you are kept fully informed in relation to new concepts, methods, practices, and directions in the field.

You discover that you are actually taking the examination all the time: you are preparing for the examination by "taking" an examination, not by reading extraneous and/or supererogatory textbooks.

In short, this PASSBOOK®, used directedly, should be an important factor in helping you to pass your test.

HOMELESS SERVICES REPRESENTATIVE III

DUTIES
As a Homeless Services Representative III, you would supervise a unit engaged in various program activities for shelters in an assigned geographic area. You would provide policy and procedural advice on conducting inspections and review inspection reports; develop and implement policies, rules, regulations and procedures concerning homeless shelter regulation with executive staff; direct provision of technical assistance to providers of shelters on operation and management issues; review existing and proposed legislation impacting homeless service programs and recommend changes; write reports for agency, gubernatorial and legislative staff on homeless shelter service issues and programs; and respond to issues and questions on policy and technical assistance. Performs related duties as required.

SCOPE OF THE EXAMINATION
The written test will cover knowledge, skills and abilities in such areas as:

1. **Preparing reports and official documents** - These questions test for the ability to prepare reports and other official documents for use within and among governmental agencies, in legal or regulatory settings, or for dissemination to the public. Some questions test for a knowledge of grammar, usage, punctuation, and sentence structure. Others test for the ability to present information clearly and accurately, to use the proper tone, and to organize paragraphs logically and comprehensibly.
2. **Administrative supervision** - These questions test for knowledge of the principles and practices involved in directing the activities of a large subordinate staff, including subordinate supervisors. Questions relate to the personal interactions between an upper level supervisor and their subordinate supervisors in the accomplishment of objectives. These questions cover such areas as assigning work to and coordinating the activities of several units, establishing and guiding staff development programs, evaluating the performance of subordinate supervisors, and maintaining relationships with other organizational sections.
3. **Understanding and applying administrative principles** - These questions test for knowledge of how to effectively manage and direct an organization or an organizational segment. These questions cover such areas as developing objectives, formulating policies, making decisions, forecasting and planning, developing personnel, organizing and coordinating work, communicating information, providing leadership, and delegating authority and responsibility.
4. **Working and interacting with others** - These questions test for knowledge of how to effectively approach work and maintain professional relationships with others in the workplace. Each question presents a situation and a number of possible approaches for handling it. Question topics may include working with supervisors and coworkers, interacting with members of the public, handling conflict, and managing workplace demands and priorities. The questions are not specific to any job title or place of work.

HOW TO TAKE A TEST

I. YOU MUST PASS AN EXAMINATION

A. WHAT EVERY CANDIDATE SHOULD KNOW

Examination applicants often ask us for help in preparing for the written test. What can I study in advance? What kinds of questions will be asked? How will the test be given? How will the papers be graded?

As an applicant for a civil service examination, you may be wondering about some of these things. Our purpose here is to suggest effective methods of advance study and to describe civil service examinations.

Your chances for success on this examination can be increased if you know how to prepare. Those "pre-examination jitters" can be reduced if you know what to expect. You can even experience an adventure in good citizenship if you know why civil service exams are given.

B. WHY ARE CIVIL SERVICE EXAMINATIONS GIVEN?

Civil service examinations are important to you in two ways. As a citizen, you want public jobs filled by employees who know how to do their work. As a job seeker, you want a fair chance to compete for that job on an equal footing with other candidates. The best-known means of accomplishing this two-fold goal is the competitive examination.

Exams are widely publicized throughout the nation. They may be administered for jobs in federal, state, city, municipal, town or village governments or agencies.

Any citizen may apply, with some limitations, such as the age or residence of applicants. Your experience and education may be reviewed to see whether you meet the requirements for the particular examination. When these requirements exist, they are reasonable and applied consistently to all applicants. Thus, a competitive examination may cause you some uneasiness now, but it is your privilege and safeguard.

C. HOW ARE CIVIL SERVICE EXAMS DEVELOPED?

Examinations are carefully written by trained technicians who are specialists in the field known as "psychological measurement," in consultation with recognized authorities in the field of work that the test will cover. These experts recommend the subject matter areas or skills to be tested; only those knowledges or skills important to your success on the job are included. The most reliable books and source materials available are used as references. Together, the experts and technicians judge the difficulty level of the questions.

Test technicians know how to phrase questions so that the problem is clearly stated. Their ethics do not permit "trick" or "catch" questions. Questions may have been tried out on sample groups, or subjected to statistical analysis, to determine their usefulness.

Written tests are often used in combination with performance tests, ratings of training and experience, and oral interviews. All of these measures combine to form the best-known means of finding the right person for the right job.

II. HOW TO PASS THE WRITTEN TEST

A. NATURE OF THE EXAMINATION

To prepare intelligently for civil service examinations, you should know how they differ from school examinations you have taken. In school you were assigned certain definite pages to read or subjects to cover. The examination questions were quite detailed and usually emphasized memory. Civil service exams, on the other hand, try to discover your present ability to perform the duties of a position, plus your potentiality to learn these duties. In other words, a civil service exam attempts to predict how successful you will be. Questions cover such a broad area that they cannot be as minute and detailed as school exam questions.

In the public service similar kinds of work, or positions, are grouped together in one "class." This process is known as *position-classification*. All the positions in a class are paid according to the salary range for that class. One class title covers all of these positions, and they are all tested by the same examination.

B. FOUR BASIC STEPS

1) Study the announcement

How, then, can you know what subjects to study? Our best answer is: "Learn as much as possible about the class of positions for which you've applied." The exam will test the knowledge, skills and abilities needed to do the work.

Your most valuable source of information about the position you want is the official exam announcement. This announcement lists the training and experience qualifications. Check these standards and apply only if you come reasonably close to meeting them.

The brief description of the position in the examination announcement offers some clues to the subjects which will be tested. Think about the job itself. Review the duties in your mind. Can you perform them, or are there some in which you are rusty? Fill in the blank spots in your preparation.

Many jurisdictions preview the written test in the exam announcement by including a section called "Knowledge and Abilities Required," "Scope of the Examination," or some similar heading. Here you will find out specifically what fields will be tested.

2) Review your own background

Once you learn in general what the position is all about, and what you need to know to do the work, ask yourself which subjects you already know fairly well and which need improvement. You may wonder whether to concentrate on improving your strong areas or on building some background in your fields of weakness. When the announcement has specified "some knowledge" or "considerable knowledge," or has used adjectives like "beginning principles of..." or "advanced ... methods," you can get a clue as to the number and difficulty of questions to be asked in any given field. More questions, and hence broader coverage, would be included for those subjects which are more important in the work. Now weigh your strengths and weaknesses against the job requirements and prepare accordingly.

3) Determine the level of the position

Another way to tell how intensively you should prepare is to understand the level of the job for which you are applying. Is it the entering level? In other words, is this the position in which beginners in a field of work are hired? Or is it an intermediate or advanced level? Sometimes this is indicated by such words as "Junior" or "Senior" in the class title. Other jurisdictions use Roman numerals to designate the level – Clerk I, Clerk II, for example. The word "Supervisor" sometimes appears in the title. If the level is not indicated by the title, check the description of duties. Will you be working under very close supervision, or will you have responsibility for independent decisions in this work?

4) Choose appropriate study materials

Now that you know the subjects to be examined and the relative amount of each subject to be covered, you can choose suitable study materials. For beginning level jobs, or even advanced ones, if you have a pronounced weakness in some aspect of your training, read a modern, standard textbook in that field. Be sure it is up to date and has general coverage. Such books are normally available at your library, and the librarian will be glad to help you locate one. For entry-level positions, questions of appropriate difficulty are chosen – neither highly advanced questions, nor those too simple. Such questions require careful thought but not advanced training.

If the position for which you are applying is technical or advanced, you will read more advanced, specialized material. If you are already familiar with the basic principles of your field, elementary textbooks would waste your time. Concentrate on advanced textbooks and technical periodicals. Think through the concepts and review difficult problems in your field.

These are all general sources. You can get more ideas on your own initiative, following these leads. For example, training manuals and publications of the government agency which employs workers in your field can be useful, particularly for technical and professional positions. A letter or visit to the government department involved may result in more specific study suggestions, and certainly will provide you with a more definite idea of the exact nature of the position you are seeking.

III. KINDS OF TESTS

Tests are used for purposes other than measuring knowledge and ability to perform specified duties. For some positions, it is equally important to test ability to make adjustments to new situations or to profit from training. In others, basic mental abilities not dependent on information are essential. Questions which test these things may not appear as pertinent to the duties of the position as those which test for knowledge and information. Yet they are often highly important parts of a fair examination. For very general questions, it is almost impossible to help you direct your study efforts. What we can do is to point out some of the more common of these general abilities needed in public service positions and describe some typical questions.

1) General information

Broad, general information has been found useful for predicting job success in some kinds of work. This is tested in a variety of ways, from vocabulary lists to questions about current events. Basic background in some field of work, such as sociology or economics, may be sampled in a group of questions. Often these are principles which have become familiar to most persons through exposure rather than through formal training. It is difficult to advise you how to study for these questions; being alert to the world around you is our best suggestion.

2) Verbal ability

An example of an ability needed in many positions is verbal or language ability. Verbal ability is, in brief, the ability to use and understand words. Vocabulary and grammar tests are typical measures of this ability. Reading comprehension or paragraph interpretation questions are common in many kinds of civil service tests. You are given a paragraph of written material and asked to find its central meaning.

3) Numerical ability

Number skills can be tested by the familiar arithmetic problem, by checking paired lists of numbers to see which are alike and which are different, or by interpreting charts and graphs. In the latter test, a graph may be printed in the test booklet which you are asked to use as the basis for answering questions.

4) Observation

A popular test for law-enforcement positions is the observation test. A picture is shown to you for several minutes, then taken away. Questions about the picture test your ability to observe both details and larger elements.

5) Following directions

In many positions in the public service, the employee must be able to carry out written instructions dependably and accurately. You may be given a chart with several columns, each column listing a variety of information. The questions require you to carry out directions involving the information given in the chart.

6) Skills and aptitudes

Performance tests effectively measure some manual skills and aptitudes. When the skill is one in which you are trained, such as typing or shorthand, you can practice. These tests are often very much like those given in business school or high school courses. For many of the other skills and aptitudes, however, no short-time preparation can be made. Skills and abilities natural to you or that you have developed throughout your lifetime are being tested.

Many of the general questions just described provide all the data needed to answer the questions and ask you to use your reasoning ability to find the answers. Your best preparation for these tests, as well as for tests of facts and ideas, is to be at your physical and mental best. You, no doubt, have your own methods of getting into an exam-taking mood and keeping "in shape." The next section lists some ideas on this subject.

IV. KINDS OF QUESTIONS

Only rarely is the "essay" question, which you answer in narrative form, used in civil service tests. Civil service tests are usually of the short-answer type. Full instructions for answering these questions will be given to you at the examination. But in case this is your first experience with short-answer questions and separate answer sheets, here is what you need to know:

1) Multiple-choice Questions

Most popular of the short-answer questions is the "multiple choice" or "best answer" question. It can be used, for example, to test for factual knowledge, ability to solve problems or judgment in meeting situations found at work.

A multiple-choice question is normally one of three types—
- It can begin with an incomplete statement followed by several possible endings. You are to find the one ending which *best* completes the statement, although some of the others may not be entirely wrong.
- It can also be a complete statement in the form of a question which is answered by choosing one of the statements listed.

- It can be in the form of a problem – again you select the best answer.

Here is an example of a multiple-choice question with a discussion which should give you some clues as to the method for choosing the right answer:

When an employee has a complaint about his assignment, the action which will *best* help him overcome his difficulty is to
- A. discuss his difficulty with his coworkers
- B. take the problem to the head of the organization
- C. take the problem to the person who gave him the assignment
- D. say nothing to anyone about his complaint

In answering this question, you should study each of the choices to find which is best. Consider choice "A" – Certainly an employee may discuss his complaint with fellow employees, but no change or improvement can result, and the complaint remains unresolved. Choice "B" is a poor choice since the head of the organization probably does not know what assignment you have been given, and taking your problem to him is known as "going over the head" of the supervisor. The supervisor, or person who made the assignment, is the person who can clarify it or correct any injustice. Choice "C" is, therefore, correct. To say nothing, as in choice "D," is unwise. Supervisors have and interest in knowing the problems employees are facing, and the employee is seeking a solution to his problem.

2) True/False Questions

The "true/false" or "right/wrong" form of question is sometimes used. Here a complete statement is given. Your job is to decide whether the statement is right or wrong.

SAMPLE: A roaming cell-phone call to a nearby city costs less than a non-roaming call to a distant city.

This statement is wrong, or false, since roaming calls are more expensive.

This is not a complete list of all possible question forms, although most of the others are variations of these common types. You will always get complete directions for answering questions. Be sure you understand *how* to mark your answers – ask questions until you do.

V. RECORDING YOUR ANSWERS

Computer terminals are used more and more today for many different kinds of exams.

For an examination with very few applicants, you may be told to record your answers in the test booklet itself. Separate answer sheets are much more common. If this separate answer sheet is to be scored by machine – and this is often the case – it is highly important that you mark your answers correctly in order to get credit.

An electronic scoring machine is often used in civil service offices because of the speed with which papers can be scored. Machine-scored answer sheets must be marked with a pencil, which will be given to you. This pencil has a high graphite content which responds to the electronic scoring machine. As a matter of fact, stray dots may register as answers, so do not let your pencil rest on the answer sheet while you are pondering the correct answer. Also, if your pencil lead breaks or is otherwise defective, ask for another.

Since the answer sheet will be dropped in a slot in the scoring machine, be careful not to bend the corners or get the paper crumpled.

The answer sheet normally has five vertical columns of numbers, with 30 numbers to a column. These numbers correspond to the question numbers in your test booklet. After each number, going across the page are four or five pairs of dotted lines. These short dotted lines have small letters or numbers above them. The first two pairs may also have a "T" or "F" above the letters. This indicates that the first two pairs only are to be used if the questions are of the true-false type. If the questions are multiple choice, disregard the "T" and "F" and pay attention only to the small letters or numbers.

Answer your questions in the manner of the sample that follows:

32. The largest city in the United States is
    A. Washington, D.C.
    B. New York City
    C. Chicago
    D. Detroit
    E. San Francisco

1) Choose the answer you think is best. (New York City is the largest, so "B" is correct.)
2) Find the row of dotted lines numbered the same as the question you are answering. (Find row number 32)
3) Find the pair of dotted lines corresponding to the answer. (Find the pair of lines under the mark "B.")
4) Make a solid black mark between the dotted lines.

VI. BEFORE THE TEST

Common sense will help you find procedures to follow to get ready for an examination. Too many of us, however, overlook these sensible measures. Indeed, nervousness and fatigue have been found to be the most serious reasons why applicants fail to do their best on civil service tests. Here is a list of reminders:

- Begin your preparation early – Don't wait until the last minute to go scurrying around for books and materials or to find out what the position is all about.
- Prepare continuously – An hour a night for a week is better than an all-night cram session. This has been definitely established. What is more, a night a week for a month will return better dividends than crowding your study into a shorter period of time.
- Locate the place of the exam – You have been sent a notice telling you when and where to report for the examination. If the location is in a different town or otherwise unfamiliar to you, it would be well to inquire the best route and learn something about the building.
- Relax the night before the test – Allow your mind to rest. Do not study at all that night. Plan some mild recreation or diversion; then go to bed early and get a good night's sleep.
- Get up early enough to make a leisurely trip to the place for the test – This way unforeseen events, traffic snarls, unfamiliar buildings, etc. will not upset you.
- Dress comfortably – A written test is not a fashion show. You will be known by number and not by name, so wear something comfortable.

- Leave excess paraphernalia at home – Shopping bags and odd bundles will get in your way. You need bring only the items mentioned in the official notice you received; usually everything you need is provided. Do not bring reference books to the exam. They will only confuse those last minutes and be taken away from you when in the test room.
- Arrive somewhat ahead of time – If because of transportation schedules you must get there very early, bring a newspaper or magazine to take your mind off yourself while waiting.
- Locate the examination room – When you have found the proper room, you will be directed to the seat or part of the room where you will sit. Sometimes you are given a sheet of instructions to read while you are waiting. Do not fill out any forms until you are told to do so; just read them and be prepared.
- Relax and prepare to listen to the instructions
- If you have any physical problem that may keep you from doing your best, be sure to tell the test administrator. If you are sick or in poor health, you really cannot do your best on the exam. You can come back and take the test some other time.

VII. AT THE TEST

The day of the test is here and you have the test booklet in your hand. The temptation to get going is very strong. Caution! There is more to success than knowing the right answers. You must know how to identify your papers and understand variations in the type of short-answer question used in this particular examination. Follow these suggestions for maximum results from your efforts:

1) Cooperate with the monitor

The test administrator has a duty to create a situation in which you can be as much at ease as possible. He will give instructions, tell you when to begin, check to see that you are marking your answer sheet correctly, and so on. He is not there to guard you, although he will see that your competitors do not take unfair advantage. He wants to help you do your best.

2) Listen to all instructions

Don't jump the gun! Wait until you understand all directions. In most civil service tests you get more time than you need to answer the questions. So don't be in a hurry. Read each word of instructions until you clearly understand the meaning. Study the examples, listen to all announcements and follow directions. Ask questions if you do not understand what to do.

3) Identify your papers

Civil service exams are usually identified by number only. You will be assigned a number; you must not put your name on your test papers. Be sure to copy your number correctly. Since more than one exam may be given, copy your exact examination title.

4) Plan your time

Unless you are told that a test is a "speed" or "rate of work" test, speed itself is usually not important. Time enough to answer all the questions will be provided, but this does not mean that you have all day. An overall time limit has been set. Divide the total time (in minutes) by the number of questions to determine the approximate time you have for each question.

5) Do not linger over difficult questions

If you come across a difficult question, mark it with a paper clip (useful to have along) and come back to it when you have been through the booklet. One caution if you do this – be sure to skip a number on your answer sheet as well. Check often to be sure that you have not lost your place and that you are marking in the row numbered the same as the question you are answering.

6) Read the questions

Be sure you know what the question asks! Many capable people are unsuccessful because they failed to *read* the questions correctly.

7) Answer all questions

Unless you have been instructed that a penalty will be deducted for incorrect answers, it is better to guess than to omit a question.

8) Speed tests

It is often better NOT to guess on speed tests. It has been found that on timed tests people are tempted to spend the last few seconds before time is called in marking answers at random – without even reading them – in the hope of picking up a few extra points. To discourage this practice, the instructions may warn you that your score will be "corrected" for guessing. That is, a penalty will be applied. The incorrect answers will be deducted from the correct ones, or some other penalty formula will be used.

9) Review your answers

If you finish before time is called, go back to the questions you guessed or omitted to give them further thought. Review other answers if you have time.

10) Return your test materials

If you are ready to leave before others have finished or time is called, take ALL your materials to the monitor and leave quietly. Never take any test material with you. The monitor can discover whose papers are not complete, and taking a test booklet may be grounds for disqualification.

VIII. EXAMINATION TECHNIQUES

1) Read the general instructions carefully. These are usually printed on the first page of the exam booklet. As a rule, these instructions refer to the timing of the examination; the fact that you should not start work until the signal and must stop work at a signal, etc. If there are any *special* instructions, such as a choice of questions to be answered, make sure that you note this instruction carefully.

2) When you are ready to start work on the examination, that is as soon as the signal has been given, read the instructions to each question booklet, underline any key words or phrases, such as *least, best, outline, describe* and the like. In this way you will tend to answer as requested rather than discover on reviewing your paper that you *listed without describing*, that you selected the *worst* choice rather than the *best* choice, etc.

3) If the examination is of the objective or multiple-choice type – that is, each question will also give a series of possible answers: A, B, C or D, and you are called upon to select the best answer and write the letter next to that answer on your answer paper – it is advisable to start answering each question in turn. There may be anywhere from 50 to 100 such questions in the three or four hours allotted and you can see how much time would be taken if you read through all the questions before beginning to answer any. Furthermore, if you come across a question or group of questions which you know would be difficult to answer, it would undoubtedly affect your handling of all the other questions.

4) If the examination is of the essay type and contains but a few questions, it is a moot point as to whether you should read all the questions before starting to answer any one. Of course, if you are given a choice – say five out of seven and the like – then it is essential to read all the questions so you can eliminate the two that are most difficult. If, however, you are asked to answer all the questions, there may be danger in trying to answer the easiest one first because you may find that you will spend too much time on it. The best technique is to answer the first question, then proceed to the second, etc.

5) Time your answers. Before the exam begins, write down the time it started, then add the time allowed for the examination and write down the time it must be completed, then divide the time available somewhat as follows:
    - If 3-1/2 hours are allowed, that would be 210 minutes. If you have 80 objective-type questions, that would be an average of 2-1/2 minutes per question. Allow yourself no more than 2 minutes per question, or a total of 160 minutes, which will permit about 50 minutes to review.
    - If for the time allotment of 210 minutes there are 7 essay questions to answer, that would average about 30 minutes a question. Give yourself only 25 minutes per question so that you have about 35 minutes to review.

6) The most important instruction is to *read each question* and make sure you know what is wanted. The second most important instruction is to *time yourself properly* so that you answer every question. The third most important instruction is to *answer every question*. Guess if you have to but include something for each question. Remember that you will receive no credit for a blank and will probably receive some credit if you write something in answer to an essay question. If you guess a letter – say "B" for a multiple-choice question – you may have guessed right. If you leave a blank as an answer to a multiple-choice question, the examiners may respect your feelings but it will not add a point to your score. Some exams may penalize you for wrong answers, so in such cases *only*, you may not want to guess unless you have some basis for your answer.

7) Suggestions
    a. Objective-type questions
        1. Examine the question booklet for proper sequence of pages and questions
        2. Read all instructions carefully
        3. Skip any question which seems too difficult; return to it after all other questions have been answered
        4. Apportion your time properly; do not spend too much time on any single question or group of questions

5. Note and underline key words – *all, most, fewest, least, best, worst, same, opposite,* etc.
6. Pay particular attention to negatives
7. Note unusual option, e.g., unduly long, short, complex, different or similar in content to the body of the question
8. Observe the use of "hedging" words – *probably, may, most likely,* etc.
9. Make sure that your answer is put next to the same number as the question
10. Do not second-guess unless you have good reason to believe the second answer is definitely more correct
11. Cross out original answer if you decide another answer is more accurate; do not erase until you are ready to hand your paper in
12. Answer all questions; guess unless instructed otherwise
13. Leave time for review

   b. Essay questions
     1. Read each question carefully
     2. Determine exactly what is wanted. Underline key words or phrases.
     3. Decide on outline or paragraph answer
     4. Include many different points and elements unless asked to develop any one or two points or elements
     5. Show impartiality by giving pros and cons unless directed to select one side only
     6. Make and write down any assumptions you find necessary to answer the questions
     7. Watch your English, grammar, punctuation and choice of words
     8. Time your answers; don't crowd material

8) Answering the essay question

Most essay questions can be answered by framing the specific response around several key words or ideas. Here are a few such key words or ideas:

M's: manpower, materials, methods, money, management
P's: purpose, program, policy, plan, procedure, practice, problems, pitfalls, personnel, public relations

   a. Six basic steps in handling problems:
     1. Preliminary plan and background development
     2. Collect information, data and facts
     3. Analyze and interpret information, data and facts
     4. Analyze and develop solutions as well as make recommendations
     5. Prepare report and sell recommendations
     6. Install recommendations and follow up effectiveness

   b. Pitfalls to avoid
     1. *Taking things for granted* – A statement of the situation does not necessarily imply that each of the elements is necessarily true; for example, a complaint may be invalid and biased so that all that can be taken for granted is that a complaint has been registered

2. *Considering only one side of a situation* – Wherever possible, indicate several alternatives and then point out the reasons you selected the best one
3. *Failing to indicate follow up* – Whenever your answer indicates action on your part, make certain that you will take proper follow-up action to see how successful your recommendations, procedures or actions turn out to be
4. *Taking too long in answering any single question* – Remember to time your answers properly

IX. AFTER THE TEST

Scoring procedures differ in detail among civil service jurisdictions although the general principles are the same. Whether the papers are hand-scored or graded by machine we have described, they are nearly always graded by number. That is, the person who marks the paper knows only the number – never the name – of the applicant. Not until all the papers have been graded will they be matched with names. If other tests, such as training and experience or oral interview ratings have been given, scores will be combined. Different parts of the examination usually have different weights. For example, the written test might count 60 percent of the final grade, and a rating of training and experience 40 percent. In many jurisdictions, veterans will have a certain number of points added to their grades.

After the final grade has been determined, the names are placed in grade order and an eligible list is established. There are various methods for resolving ties between those who get the same final grade – probably the most common is to place first the name of the person whose application was received first. Job offers are made from the eligible list in the order the names appear on it. You will be notified of your grade and your rank as soon as all these computations have been made. This will be done as rapidly as possible.

People who are found to meet the requirements in the announcement are called "eligibles." Their names are put on a list of eligible candidates. An eligible's chances of getting a job depend on how high he stands on this list and how fast agencies are filling jobs from the list.

When a job is to be filled from a list of eligibles, the agency asks for the names of people on the list of eligibles for that job. When the civil service commission receives this request, it sends to the agency the names of the three people highest on this list. Or, if the job to be filled has specialized requirements, the office sends the agency the names of the top three persons who meet these requirements from the general list.

The appointing officer makes a choice from among the three people whose names were sent to him. If the selected person accepts the appointment, the names of the others are put back on the list to be considered for future openings.

That is the rule in hiring from all kinds of eligible lists, whether they are for typist, carpenter, chemist, or something else. For every vacancy, the appointing officer has his choice of any one of the top three eligibles on the list. This explains why the person whose name is on top of the list sometimes does not get an appointment when some of the persons lower on the list do. If the appointing officer chooses the second or third eligible, the No. 1 eligible does not get a job at once, but stays on the list until he is appointed or the list is terminated.

X. HOW TO PASS THE INTERVIEW TEST

The examination for which you applied requires an oral interview test. You have already taken the written test and you are now being called for the interview test – the final part of the formal examination.

You may think that it is not possible to prepare for an interview test and that there are no procedures to follow during an interview. Our purpose is to point out some things you can do in advance that will help you and some good rules to follow and pitfalls to avoid while you are being interviewed.

What is an interview supposed to test?

The written examination is designed to test the technical knowledge and competence of the candidate; the oral is designed to evaluate intangible qualities, not readily measured otherwise, and to establish a list showing the relative fitness of each candidate – as measured against his competitors – for the position sought. Scoring is not on the basis of "right" and "wrong," but on a sliding scale of values ranging from "not passable" to "outstanding." As a matter of fact, it is possible to achieve a relatively low score without a single "incorrect" answer because of evident weakness in the qualities being measured.

Occasionally, an examination may consist entirely of an oral test – either an individual or a group oral. In such cases, information is sought concerning the technical knowledges and abilities of the candidate, since there has been no written examination for this purpose. More commonly, however, an oral test is used to supplement a written examination.

Who conducts interviews?

The composition of oral boards varies among different jurisdictions. In nearly all, a representative of the personnel department serves as chairman. One of the members of the board may be a representative of the department in which the candidate would work. In some cases, "outside experts" are used, and, frequently, a businessman or some other representative of the general public is asked to serve. Labor and management or other special groups may be represented. The aim is to secure the services of experts in the appropriate field.

However the board is composed, it is a good idea (and not at all improper or unethical) to ascertain in advance of the interview who the members are and what groups they represent. When you are introduced to them, you will have some idea of their backgrounds and interests, and at least you will not stutter and stammer over their names.

What should be done before the interview?

While knowledge about the board members is useful and takes some of the surprise element out of the interview, there is other preparation which is more substantive. It *is* possible to prepare for an oral interview – in several ways:

1) Keep a copy of your application and review it carefully before the interview

This may be the only document before the oral board, and the starting point of the interview. Know what education and experience you have listed there, and the sequence and dates of all of it. Sometimes the board will ask you to review the highlights of your experience for them; you should not have to hem and haw doing it.

2) Study the class specification and the examination announcement

Usually, the oral board has one or both of these to guide them. The qualities, characteristics or knowledges required by the position sought are stated in these documents. They offer valuable clues as to the nature of the oral interview. For example, if the job involves supervisory responsibilities, the announcement will usually indicate that knowledge of modern supervisory methods and the qualifications of the candidate as a supervisor will be tested. If so, you can expect such questions, frequently in the form of a hypothetical situation which you are expected to solve. NEVER go into an oral without knowledge of the duties and responsibilities of the job you seek.

3) Think through each qualification required

Try to visualize the kind of questions you would ask if you were a board member. How well could you answer them? Try especially to appraise your own knowledge and background in each area, *measured against the job sought*, and identify any areas in which you are weak. Be critical and realistic – do not flatter yourself.

4) Do some general reading in areas in which you feel you may be weak

For example, if the job involves supervision and your past experience has NOT, some general reading in supervisory methods and practices, particularly in the field of human relations, might be useful. Do NOT study agency procedures or detailed manuals. The oral board will be testing your understanding and capacity, not your memory.

5) Get a good night's sleep and watch your general health and mental attitude

You will want a clear head at the interview. Take care of a cold or any other minor ailment, and of course, no hangovers.

What should be done on the day of the interview?

Now comes the day of the interview itself. Give yourself plenty of time to get there. Plan to arrive somewhat ahead of the scheduled time, particularly if your appointment is in the fore part of the day. If a previous candidate fails to appear, the board might be ready for you a bit early. By early afternoon an oral board is almost invariably behind schedule if there are many candidates, and you may have to wait. Take along a book or magazine to read, or your application to review, but leave any extraneous material in the waiting room when you go in for your interview. In any event, relax and compose yourself.

The matter of dress is important. The board is forming impressions about you – from your experience, your manners, your attitude, and your appearance. Give your personal appearance careful attention. Dress your best, but not your flashiest. Choose conservative, appropriate clothing, and be sure it is immaculate. This is a business interview, and your appearance should indicate that you regard it as such. Besides, being well groomed and properly dressed will help boost your confidence.

Sooner or later, someone will call your name and escort you into the interview room. *This is it.* From here on you are on your own. It is too late for any more preparation. But remember, you asked for this opportunity to prove your fitness, and you are here because your request was granted.

What happens when you go in?

The usual sequence of events will be as follows: The clerk (who is often the board stenographer) will introduce you to the chairman of the oral board, who will introduce you to the other members of the board. Acknowledge the introductions before you sit down. Do not be surprised if you find a microphone facing you or a stenotypist sitting by. Oral interviews are usually recorded in the event of an appeal or other review.

Usually the chairman of the board will open the interview by reviewing the highlights of your education and work experience from your application – primarily for the benefit of the other members of the board, as well as to get the material into the record. Do not interrupt or comment unless there is an error or significant misinterpretation; if that is the case, do not hesitate. But do not quibble about insignificant matters. Also, he will usually ask you some question about your education, experience or your present job – partly to get you to start talking and to establish the interviewing "rapport." He may start the actual questioning, or turn it over to one of the other members. Frequently, each member undertakes the questioning on a particular area, one in which he is perhaps most competent, so you can expect each member to participate in the examination. Because time is limited, you may also expect some rather abrupt switches in the direction the questioning takes, so do not be upset by it. Normally, a board member will not pursue a single line of questioning unless he discovers a particular strength or weakness.

After each member has participated, the chairman will usually ask whether any member has any further questions, then will ask you if you have anything you wish to add. Unless you are expecting this question, it may floor you. Worse, it may start you off on an extended, extemporaneous speech. The board is not usually seeking more information. The question is principally to offer you a last opportunity to present further qualifications or to indicate that you have nothing to add. So, if you feel that a significant qualification or characteristic has been overlooked, it is proper to point it out in a sentence or so. Do not compliment the board on the thoroughness of their examination – they have been sketchy, and you know it. If you wish, merely say, "No thank you, I have nothing further to add." This is a point where you can "talk yourself out" of a good impression or fail to present an important bit of information. Remember, *you close the interview yourself.*

The chairman will then say, "That is all, Mr. _____, thank you." Do not be startled; the interview is over, and quicker than you think. Thank him, gather your belongings and take your leave. Save your sigh of relief for the other side of the door.

How to put your best foot forward

Throughout this entire process, you may feel that the board individually and collectively is trying to pierce your defenses, seek out your hidden weaknesses and embarrass and confuse you. Actually, this is not true. They are obliged to make an appraisal of your qualifications for the job you are seeking, and they want to see you in your best light. Remember, they must interview all candidates and a non-cooperative candidate may become a failure in spite of their best efforts to bring out his qualifications. Here are 15 suggestions that will help you:

1) Be natural – Keep your attitude confident, not cocky

If you are not confident that you can do the job, do not expect the board to be. Do not apologize for your weaknesses, try to bring out your strong points. The board is interested in a positive, not negative, presentation. Cockiness will antagonize any board member and make him wonder if you are covering up a weakness by a false show of strength.

2) Get comfortable, but don't lounge or sprawl

Sit erectly but not stiffly. A careless posture may lead the board to conclude that you are careless in other things, or at least that you are not impressed by the importance of the occasion. Either conclusion is natural, even if incorrect. Do not fuss with your clothing, a pencil or an ashtray. Your hands may occasionally be useful to emphasize a point; do not let them become a point of distraction.

3) Do not wisecrack or make small talk

This is a serious situation, and your attitude should show that you consider it as such. Further, the time of the board is limited – they do not want to waste it, and neither should you.

4) Do not exaggerate your experience or abilities

In the first place, from information in the application or other interviews and sources, the board may know more about you than you think. Secondly, you probably will not get away with it. An experienced board is rather adept at spotting such a situation, so do not take the chance.

5) If you know a board member, do not make a point of it, yet do not hide it

Certainly you are not fooling him, and probably not the other members of the board. Do not try to take advantage of your acquaintanceship – it will probably do you little good.

6) Do not dominate the interview

Let the board do that. They will give you the clues – do not assume that you have to do all the talking. Realize that the board has a number of questions to ask you, and do not try to take up all the interview time by showing off your extensive knowledge of the answer to the first one.

7) Be attentive

You only have 20 minutes or so, and you should keep your attention at its sharpest throughout. When a member is addressing a problem or question to you, give him your undivided attention. Address your reply principally to him, but do not exclude the other board members.

8) Do not interrupt

A board member may be stating a problem for you to analyze. He will ask you a question when the time comes. Let him state the problem, and wait for the question.

9) Make sure you understand the question

Do not try to answer until you are sure what the question is. If it is not clear, restate it in your own words or ask the board member to clarify it for you. However, do not haggle about minor elements.

10) Reply promptly but not hastily

A common entry on oral board rating sheets is "candidate responded readily," or "candidate hesitated in replies." Respond as promptly and quickly as you can, but do not jump to a hasty, ill-considered answer.

11) Do not be peremptory in your answers

A brief answer is proper – but do not fire your answer back. That is a losing game from your point of view. The board member can probably ask questions much faster than you can answer them.

12) Do not try to create the answer you think the board member wants

He is interested in what kind of mind you have and how it works – not in playing games. Furthermore, he can usually spot this practice and will actually grade you down on it.

13) Do not switch sides in your reply merely to agree with a board member

Frequently, a member will take a contrary position merely to draw you out and to see if you are willing and able to defend your point of view. Do not start a debate, yet do not surrender a good position. If a position is worth taking, it is worth defending.

14) Do not be afraid to admit an error in judgment if you are shown to be wrong

The board knows that you are forced to reply without any opportunity for careful consideration. Your answer may be demonstrably wrong. If so, admit it and get on with the interview.

15) Do not dwell at length on your present job

The opening question may relate to your present assignment. Answer the question but do not go into an extended discussion. You are being examined for a *new* job, not your present one. As a matter of fact, try to phrase ALL your answers in terms of the job for which you are being examined.

Basis of Rating

Probably you will forget most of these "do's" and "don'ts" when you walk into the oral interview room. Even remembering them all will not ensure you a passing grade. Perhaps you did not have the qualifications in the first place. But remembering them will help you to put your best foot forward, without treading on the toes of the board members.

Rumor and popular opinion to the contrary notwithstanding, an oral board wants you to make the best appearance possible. They know you are under pressure – but they also want to see how you respond to it as a guide to what your reaction would be under the pressures of the job you seek. They will be influenced by the degree of poise you display, the personal traits you show and the manner in which you respond.

ABOUT THIS BOOK

This book contains tests divided into Examination Sections. Go through each test, answering every question in the margin. We have also attached a sample answer sheet at the back of the book that can be removed and used. At the end of each test look at the answer key and check your answers. On the ones you got wrong, look at the right answer choice and learn. Do not fill in the answers first. Do not memorize the questions and answers, but understand the answer and principles involved. On your test, the questions will likely be different from the samples. Questions are changed and new ones added. If you understand these past questions you should have success with any changes that arise. Tests may consist of several types of questions. We have additional books on each subject should more study be advisable or necessary for you. Finally, the more you study, the better prepared you will be. This book is intended to be the last thing you study before you walk into the examination room. Prior study of relevant texts is also recommended. NLC publishes some of these in our Fundamental Series. Knowledge and good sense are important factors in passing your exam. Good luck also helps. So now study this Passbook, absorb the material contained within and take that knowledge into the examination. Then do your best to pass that exam.

EXAMINATION SECTION

EXAMINATION SECTION
TEST 1

DIRECTIONS: Each question or incomplete statement is followed by several suggested answers or completions. Select the one that BEST answers the question or completes the statement. *PRINT THE LETTER OF THE CORRECT ANSWER IN THE SPACE AT THE RIGHT.*

1. When conducting a needs assessment for the purpose of education planning, an agency's FIRST step is to identify or provide
    A. a profile of population characteristics
    B. barriers to participation
    C. existing resources
    D. profiles of competing resources

    1.____

2. Research has demonstrated that of the following, the MOST effective medium for communicating with external publics is(are)
    A. video news releases   B. television
    C. radio   D. newspapers

    2.____

3. Basic ideas behind the effort to influence the attitudes and behaviors of a constituency include each of the following EXCEPT the idea that
    A. words, rather than actions or events, are most likely to motivate
    B. demands for action are a usual response
    C. self-interest usually figures heavily into public involvement
    D. the reliability of change programs is difficult to assess

    3.____

4. An agency representative is trying to craft a pithy message to constituents in order to encourage the use of agency program resources.
   Choosing an audience for such messages is easiest when the message
    A. is project- or behavior-based   B. is combined with other messages
    C. is abstract   D. has a broad appeal

    4.____

5. Of the following factors, the MOST important to the success of an agency's external education or communication programs is the
    A. amount of resources used to implement them
    B. public's prior experiences with the agency
    C. real value of the program to the public
    D. commitment of the internal audience

    5.____

6. A representative for a state agency is being interviewed by a reporter from a local news network. The representative is being asked to defend a program that is extremely unpopular in certain parts of the municipality.
   When a constituency is known to be opposed to a position, the MOST useful communication strategy is to present

    6.____

A. only the arguments that are consistent with constituents' views
B. only the agency's side of the issue
C. both sides of the argument as clearly as possible
D. both sides of the argument, omitting key information about the opposing position

7. The MOST significant barriers to effective agency community relations include
   I. widespread distrust of communication strategies
   II. the media's "watchdog" stance
   III. public apathy
   IV. statutory opposition

   The CORRECT answer is:
   A. I only   B. I and II   C. II and III   D. III and IV

8. In conducting an education program, many agencies use workshops and seminars in a classroom setting.
   Advantages of classroom-style teaching over other means of educating the public include each of the following, EXCEPT
   A. enabling an instructor to verify learning through testing and interaction with the target audience
   B. enabling hands-on practice and other participatory learning techniques
   C. ability to reach an unlimited number of participants in a given length of time
   D. ability to convey the latest, most up-to-date information

9. The _____ model of community relations is characterized by an attempt to persuade the public to adopt the agency's point of view.
   A. two-way symmetric   B. two-way asymmetric
   C. public information   D. press agency/publicity

10. Important elements of an internal situation analysis include the
    I. list of agency opponents   II. communication audit
    III. updated organizational almanac   IV. stakeholder analysis

    The CORRECT answer is:
    A. I and II   B. I, II, and III   C. II and III   D. I, II, III and IV

11. Government agency information efforts typically involve each of the following objectives, EXCEPT to
    A. implement changes in the policies of government agencies to align with public opinion
    B. communicate the work of agencies
    C. explain agency techniques in a way that invites input from citizens
    D. provide citizen feedback to government administrators

12. Factors that are likely to influence the effectiveness of an educational campaign include the
    I. level of homogeneity among intended participants
    II. number and types of media used
    III. receptivity of the intended participants
    IV. level of specificity in the message or behavior to be taught

    The CORRECT answer is:
    A. I and II   B. I, II, and III   C. II and III   D. I, II, III, and IV

13. An agency representative is writing instructional objectives that will later help to measure the effectiveness of an educational program.
    Which of the following verbs, included in an objective, would be MOST helpful for the purpose of measuring effectiveness?
    A. Know   B. Identify   C. Learn   D. Comprehend

14. A state education agency wants to encourage participation in a program that has just received a boost through new federal legislation. The program is intended to include participants from a wide variety of socioeconomic and other demographic characteristics. The agency wants to launch a broad-based program that will inform virtually every interested party in the state about the program's new circumstances.
    In attempting to deliver this message to such a wide-ranging constituency, the agency's BEST practice would be to
    A. broadcast the same message through as many different media channels as possible
    B. focus on one discrete segment of the public at a time
    C. craft a message whose appeal is as broad as the public itself
    D. let the program's achievements speak for themselves and rely on word-of-mouth

15. Advantages associated with using the World Wide Web as an educational tool include
    I. an appeal to younger generations of the public
    II. visually-oriented, interactive learning
    III. learning that is not confined by space, time, or institutional association
    IV. a variety of methods for verifying use and learning

    The CORRECT answer is:
    A. I only   B. I and II   C. I, II, and III   D. I, II, II, and IV

16. In agencies involved in health care, community relations is a critical function because it
    A. serves as an intermediary between the agency and consumers
    B. generates a clear mission statement for agency goals and priorities
    C. ensures patient privacy while satisfying the media's right to information
    D. helps marketing professionals determine the wants and needs of agency constituents

17. After an extensive campaign to promote its newest program to constituents, an agency learns that most of the audience did not understand the intended message.
    MOST likely, the agency has
    A. chosen words that were intended to inform, rather than persuade
    B. not accurately interpreted what the audience really needed to know
    C. overestimated the ability of the audience to receive and process the message
    D. compensated for noise that may have interrupted the message

17.____

18. The necessary elements that lead to conviction and motivation in the minds of participants in an educational or information program include each of the following, EXCEPT the _____ of the message.
    A. acceptability   B. intensity
    C. single-channel appeal   D. pervasiveness

18.____

19. Printed materials are often at the core of educational programs provided by public agencies.
    The PRIMARY disadvantage associated with print is that it
    A. does not enable comprehensive treatment of a topic
    B. is generally unreliable in term of assessing results
    C. is often the most expensive medium available
    D. is constrained by time

19.____

20. Traditional thinking on public opinion holds that there is about _____ percent of the public who are pivotal to shifting the balance and momentum of opinion—they are concerned about an issue, but not fanatical, and interested enough to pay attention to a reasoned discussion.
    A. 2   B. 10   C. 33   D. 51

20.____

21. One of the most useful guidelines for influencing attitude change among people is to
    A. invite the target audience to come to you, rather than approaching them
    B. use moral appeals as the primary approach
    C. use concrete images to enable people to see the results of behaviors or indifference
    D. offer tangible rewards to people for changes in behavior

21.____

22. An agency is attempting to evaluate the effectiveness of its educational program. For this purpose, it wants to observe several focus groups discussing the same program.
    Which of the following would NOT be a guideline for the use of focus groups?
    A. Focus groups should only include those who have participated in the program.
    B. Be sure to accurately record the discussion.
    C. The same questions should be asked at each focus group meeting.
    D. It is often helpful to have a neutral, non-agency employee facilitate discussions.

22.____

23. Research consistently shows that _____ is the determinant most likely to make a newspaper editor run a news release.
    A. novelty   B. prominence   C. proximity   D. conflict

24. Which of the following is NOT one of the major variables to take into account when considering a population-needs assessment?
    A. State of program development   B. Resources available
    C. Demographics   D. Community attitudes

25. The FIRST step in any communications audit is to
    A. develop a research instrument
    B. determine how the organization currently communicates
    C. hire a contractor
    D. determine which audience to assess

KEY (CORRECT ANSWERS)

1. A
2. D
3. A
4. A
5. D

6. C
7. D
8. C
9. B
10. C

11. A
12. D
13. B
14. B
15. C

16. A
17. B
18. C
19. B
20. B

21. C
22. A
23. C
24. C
25. D

TEST 2

DIRECTIONS: Each question or incomplete statement is followed by several suggested answers or completions. Select the one that BEST answers the question or completes the statement. *PRINT THE LETTER OF THE CORRECT ANSWER IN THE SPACE AT THE RIGHT.*

1. A public relations practitioner at an agency has just composed a press release highlighting a program's recent accomplishments and success stories.
   In pitching such releases to print outlets, the practitioner should
   I. e-mail, mail, or send them by messenger
   II. address them to "editor" or "news director"
   III. have an assistant call all media contacts by telephone
   IV. ask reporters or editors how they prefer to receive them

   The CORRECT answer is:
   A. I and II   B. I and IV   C. II, III, and IV   D. III only

2. The "output goals" of an educational program are MOST likely to include
   A. specified ratings of services by participants on a standardized scale
   B. observable effects on a given community or clientele
   C. the number of instructional hours provided
   D. the number of participants served

3. An agency wants to evaluate satisfaction levels among program participants, and mails out questionnaires to everyone who has been enrolled in the last year.
   The PRIMARY problem associated with this method of evaluative research is that it
   A. poses a significant inconvenience for respondents
   B. is inordinately expensive
   C. does not allow for follow-up or clarification questions
   D. usually involves a low response rate

4. A communications audit is an important tool for measuring
   A. the depth of penetration of a particular message or program
   B. the cost of the organization's information campaigns
   C. how key audiences perceive an organization
   D. the commitment of internal stakeholders

5. The "ABCs" of written learning objectives include each of the following, EXCEPT
   A. Audience   B. Behavior   C. Conditions   D. Delineation

6. When attempting to change the behaviors of constituents, it is important to keep in mind that
   I. most people are skeptical of communications that try to get them to change their behaviors
   II. in most cases, a person selects the media to which he exposes himself
   III. people tend to react defensively to messages or programs that rely on fear as a motivating factor
   IV. programs should aim for the broadest appeal possible in order to include as many participants as possible

   The CORRECT answer is:
   A. I and II   B. I, II and III   C. II and III   D. I, II, III, and IV

7. The "laws" of public opinion include the idea that it is
   A. useful for anticipating emergencies
   B. not sensitive to important events
   C. basically determined by self-interest
   D. sustainable through persistent appeals

8. Which of the following types of evaluations is used to measure public attitudes before and after an information/educational program?
   A. Retrieval study
   B. Copy test
   C. Quota sampling
   D. Benchmark study

9. The PRIMARY source for internal communications is(are) usually
   A. flow charts
   B. meetings
   C. voice mail
   D. printed publications

10. An agency representative is putting together informational materials—brochures and a newsletter—outlining changes in one of the state's biggest benefits programs.
    In assembling print materials as a medium for delivering information to the public, the representative should keep in mind each of the following trends:
    I. For various reasons, the reading capabilities of the public are in general decline
    II. Without tables and graphs to help illustrate the changes, it is unlikely that the message will be delivered effectively
    III. Professionals and career-oriented people are highly receptive to information written in the form of a journal article or empirical study
    IV. People tend to be put off by print materials that use itemized and bulleted (●) lists

    The CORRECT answer is:
    A. I and II   B. I, II and III   C. II and III   D. I, II, III, and IV

11. Which of the following steps in a problem-oriented information campaign would typically be implemented FIRST?
    A. Deciding on tactics
    B. Determining a communications strategy
    C. Evaluating the problem's impact
    D. Developing an organizational strategy

12. A common pitfall in conducting an educational program is to
    A. aim it at the wrong target audience
    B. overfund it
    C. leave it in the hands of people who are in the business of education, rather than those with expertise in the business of the organization
    D. ignore the possibility that some other organization is meeting the same educational need for the target audience

13. The key factors that affect the credibility of an agency's educational program include
    A. organization
    B. scope
    C. sophistication
    D. penetration

14. Research on public opinion consistently demonstrates that it is
    A. easy to move people toward a strong opinion on anything, as long as they are approached directly through their emotions
    B. easier to move people away from an opinion they currently hold than to have them form an opinion about something they have not previously cared about
    C. easy to move people toward a strong opinion on anything, as long as the message appeals to their reason and intellect
    D. difficult to move people toward a strong opinion on anything, no matter what the approach

15. In conducting an education program, many agencies use meetings and conferences to educate an audience about the organization and its programs. Advantages associated with this approach include
    I. a captive audience that is known to be interested in the topic
    II. ample opportunities for verifying learning
    III. cost-efficient meeting space
    IV. the ability to provide information on a wider variety of subjects

    The CORRECT answer is:
    A. I and II   B. I, III and IV   C. II and III   D. I, II, III and IV

16. An agency is attempting to evaluate the effectiveness of its educational programs. For this purpose, it wants to observe several focus groups discussing particular programs.
    For this purpose, a focus group should never number more than _____ participants.
    A. 5   B. 10   C. 15   D. 20

17. A _____ speech is written so that several agency members can deliver it to different audiences with only minor variations.
   A. basic   B. printed   C. quota   D. pattern

18. Which of the following statements about public opinion is generally considered to be FALSE?
   A. Opinion is primarily reactive rather than proactive.
   B. People have more opinions about goals than about the means by which to achieve them.
   C. Facts tend to shift opinion in the accepted direction when opinion is not solidly structured.
   D. Public opinion is based more on information than desire.

19. An agency is trying to promote its educational program.
    As a general rule, the agency should NOT assume that
   A. people will only participate if they perceive an individual benefit
   B. promotions need to be aimed at small, discrete groups
   C. if the program is good, the audience will find out about it
   D. a variety of methods, including advertising, special events, and direct mail, should be considered

20. In planning a successful educational program, probably the first and most important question for an agency to ask is:
   A. What will be the content of the program?
   B. Who will be served by the program?
   C. When is the best time to schedule the program?
   D. Why is the program necessary?

21. Media kits are LEAST likely to contain
   A. fact sheets   B. memoranda
   C. photographs with captions   D. news releases

22. The use of pamphlets and booklets as media for communication with the public often involves the disadvantage that
   A. the messages contained within them are frequently nonspecific
   B. it is difficult to measure their effectiveness in delivering the message
   C. there are few opportunities for people to refer to them
   D. color reproduction is poor

23. The MOST important prerequisite of a good educational program is an
   A. abundance of resources to implement it
   B. individual staff unit formed for the purpose of program delivery
   C. accurate needs assessment
   D. uneducated constituency

24. After an education program has been delivered, an agency conducts a program evaluation to determine whether its objectives have been met.
General rules about how to conduct such an education program valuation include each of the following, EXCEPT that it
    A. must be done immediately after the program has been implemented
    B. should be simple and easy to use
    C. should be designed so that tabulation of responses can take place quickly and inexpensively
    D. should solicit mostly subjective, open-ended responses if the audience was large

25. Using electronic media such as television as means of educating the public is typically recommended ONLY for agencies that
    I. have a fairly simple message to begin with
    II. want to reach the masses, rather than a targeted audience
    III. have substantial financial resources
    IV. accept that they will not be able to measure the results of the campaign with much precision

    The CORRECT answer is:
       A. I and II   B. I, II and III   C. II and IV   D. I, II, III and IV

KEY (CORRECT ANSWERS)

1.	B	11.	C
2.	C	12.	D
3.	D	13.	A
4.	C	14.	D
5.	D	15.	B
6.	B	16.	B
7.	C	17.	D
8.	D	18.	D
9.	D	19.	C
10.	A	20.	D

21.	B
22.	B
23.	C
24.	D
25.	D

EXAMINATION SECTION

TEST 1

DIRECTIONS: Each question or incomplete statement is followed by several suggested answers or completions. Select the one that BEST answers the question or completes the statement. *PRINT THE LETTER OF THE CORRECT ANSWER IN THE SPACE AT THE RIGHT.*

1. A specialist is meeting with a panel of local community leaders to determine their perceptions about the effectiveness of a recent outreach program. The leaders seem unresponsive to the specialist's questions, looking at the floor or each other without directly answering the specialist's questions.
   One strategy that might work to elicit the desired information would be to
   A. try to discern the hidden meaning of their silence
   B. adopt a mildly confrontational tone and remind them of what's at stake in the community
   C. keep asking open-ended questions and wait patiently for responses
   D. tell them to come back when they're ready to tell you their opinions

   1.____

2. Each of the following statements about maintaining a community's attention is true, EXCEPT:
   A. The more challenging it is to pay attention to a message, the more likely it is that it will be attended to
   B. Listeners will be more motivated to pay attention if a speech is personally meaningful
   C. People will be more likely to attend if a speaker pauses to suggest natural transitions in a speech
   D. Listeners will attend to messages that stand out

   2.____

3. Each of the following is a key strategy to integrative bargaining among community members in conflict, EXCEPT
   A. focusing on positions, rather than interests
   B. separating the people from the problem
   C. aiming for an outcome based on an objectively identified standard
   D. using active listening skills, such as rephrasing and questioning

   3.____

4. Which of the following is NOT one of the major variables to take into account when considering a community needs assessment?
   A. State of program development   B. Resources available
   C. Demographics   D. Community attitudes

   4.____

5. Which of the following groups would probably be formed specifically for, or be involved in, the purpose of addressing a specific unmet community need?
   A. An existing consumer group
   B. A council of community representatives
   C. A committee
   D. An existing community organization

   5.____

6. If a public outreach campaign designed to mobilize a community fails, the MOST likely reason for this failure is that the campaign
   A. was not specific about what it wanted people to do
   B. was overly serious and did not appeal to people's sense of humor
   C. offered no incentive for the audience to make a change
   D. did not use language that appealed to the audience's emotions

7. Nationwide, the rate of involvement of elderly people in community-based programs demonstrates that they are
   A. under-served when compared to other age groups
   B. served at about the same rate as other age groups
   C. over-served when compared to other age groups
   D. hardly served at all

8. In projecting the likelihood of an education program's success, a domestic violence specialist identifies every single event that must occur to complete the project. The specialist then arranges these events in sequential order and allocates time requirements for each. Finally, the total time is calculated and a model showing all their events and timelines is charted.
   The specialist has used
   A. a PERT chart
   B. a simulation
   C. a Markov model
   D. the critical path method

9. When working with members of a predominantly African-American community, specialists from other cultural backgrounds should be aware that African-Americans tend to express thoughts and feelings through descriptions of
   A. physically tangible sensations
   B. problems to be analyzed
   C. corresponding analogies
   D. spiritual issues

10. Local nonprofessionals should be considered useful to a specialist who is looking to undertake a community outreach or educational initiative.
    Which of the following is LEAST likely to be a characteristic or role demonstrated by these community members?
    A. Undertaking support functions at the agency
    B. Serving as a communication channel between the agency and clients
    C. Encouraging greater agency acceptance and credibility within the community
    D. Helping the agency to accomplish meaningful change

11. In working with Native American groups or clients, it is important to recognize that the GREATEST health problem facing their communities today is
    A. domestic violence
    B. depression and suicide
    C. alcoholism
    D. tuberculosis

12. A specialist is facilitating a cooperative conflict resolution session between community members who have different opinions about what kinds of intervention services should be offered by the local adult protective services agency.
    Which of the following is NOT a guideline that should be followed in this process?
    A. Early in the negotiations, ask each party to name the issues on which they will positively not yield.
    B. Try to get the parties to view the issue from other points of view, beside the two or three conflicting ones.
    C. Have each side volunteer what it would be willing to do to resolve the conflict.
    D. At the end of the session, draw up a formal agreement with agreed-upon actions for both parties.

12.____

13. A specialist wants to evaluate the effectiveness of a local women's shelter. The shelter has suffered from lax participation, given the number of women who have been abused in the surrounding area. The specialist wants to speak with the women in the community who did not follow up on referrals to the shelter, and begins by visiting some of these women. After gaining the trust of these women, the specialist asks for the names of women they know who might be in need of help with a domestic violence situation.
    The specialist's approach in this case is _____ sampling.
    A. maximum variation   B. snowball
    C. convenience   D. typical case

13.____

14. When it comes to perceiving messages, people typically DON'T
    A. tend to simplify causal connections and sometimes even seek a single cause to explain what may be a highly complex effect
    B. tend to perceive messages independently of a categorical framework, especially if the message may be distorted by such an interpretation
    C. have a predisposition toward accepting any pattern that a speaker offers to explain seemingly unconnected facts
    D. tend to interpret things in the way they are viewed by their reference group

14.____

15. The elder members of Native American communities, regardless of kinship, are MOST commonly referred to as
    A. the ancients   B. father or mother
    C. grandfather or grandmother D. chiefs

15.____

16. Each of the following is typically an objective of community mobilization, EXCEPT:
    A. To convince existing community resources to alter their services or work together to address an unmet need
    B. To gather and distribute information to consumers and agencies about unmet needs

16.____

C. To publicize existing community resources and make them more accessible
D. To bring an unmet community need to public attention in order to achieve acceptance of and support for fulfilling the need

17. Research in community outreach shows that women often build friendships through shared positive feelings, whereas men often build friendships through
    A. metacommunication
    B. catharsis
    C. impression management
    D. shared activities

18. Typically, the FIRST step in a community-needs assessment is to
    A. identify community's strengths
    B. explore the nature of the neighborhood
    C. get to know the area and its residents
    D. talk to people in the community

19. Most public relations experts agree that _____ exposure(s) to a message is the minimum just to get the message noticed. If the aim of a public outreach campaign is action or a change in behavior, the agency budget must plan for more exposures.
    A. one
    B. two
    C. three
    D. four

20. In the program development/community liaison model of community work and public outreach, the PRIMARY constituency is considered to be
    A. community representatives and the service agency board or administrators
    B. elected officials, social agencies, and interagency organizations
    C. marginalized or oppressed population groups in a city or region
    D. residents of a neighborhood, parish or rural county

21. Social or interpersonal problems in many African-American communities have their roots in
    A. personality deficits
    B. unresolved family conflicts
    C. poor communication
    D. external stressors

22. A public outreach campaign should
    I. focus on short-term, measurable goals, rather than ultimate outcomes
    II. try to alter entrenched attitudes within a short time, with powerfully worded messages
    III. proceed in steps or phases, each of which lays out a mechanism that leads to the desired effect
    IV. ignore causes that led to a problem, and instead focus on solutions

    The CORRECT answer is:
    A. I and II
    B. II and III
    C. III only
    D. I, II, III and IV

23. Research findings indicate that in listing preferences for helping professional attributes, individuals from culturally diverse groups are MOST likely to consider _____ as more important than _____.
    A. personality similarity; either race/ethnic similarity or attitude similarity
    B. therapist experience; any kind of similarity
    C. race/ethnic similarity; attitude similarity
    D. attitude similarity; race/ethnic similarity

24. Each of the following is considered to be an objective of community organization EXCEPT
    A. effecting changes in the distribution of decision-making power
    B. helping people develop and strengthen the traits of self-direction and cooperation
    C. effecting and maintaining the balance between needs and resources in a community
    D. helping people deal with their problems by developing alternative behaviors

25. A specialist is helping the adult protective services agency to design a public outreach campaign. The topic to be addressed is complex, public understanding is low, and most professionals at the agency feel that having more complete information might change the opinions of community members. Which method of pre-campaign research is probably MOST appropriate?
    A. Deliberative polling
    B. Attitude scales
    C. Surveys or questionnaires
    D. Focus groups

KEY (CORRECT ANSWERS)

1.	C	11.	C
2.	A	12.	A
3.	A	13.	B
4.	C	14.	B
5.	C	15.	C
6.	A	16.	B
7.	A	17.	D
8.	D	18.	B
9.	C	19.	C
10.	A	20.	A

21. D
22. C
23. D
24. D
25. A

TEST 2

DIRECTIONS: Each question or incomplete statement is followed by several suggested answers or completions. Select the one that BEST answers the question or completes the statement. *PRINT THE LETTER OF THE CORRECT ANSWER IN THE SPACE AT THE RIGHT.*

1. A specialist has been called in to resolve a dispute between two community leaders who have been arguing about the level of service needed within the community. The discussion has been going on for several hours when the specialist arrives, and both people seem to be upset.
After calming the two down and getting each of them to agree on a statement of the problem, the specialist should ask each person to
   A. summarize his or her argument in three main points
   B. explain why he or she became so upset
   C. clearly state, in objective terms, the position of the other in a form that meets with the other's approval
   D. identify the best alternative outcome, other than their presumed ideal

1.____

2. In evaluating the impact of a public outreach campaign, the _____ model can be used early in the campaign to address first impressions.
   A. exposure or advertising
   B. expert interview
   C. impact monitoring or process
   D. experimental or quasi-experimental

2.____

3. When trying to motivate an older population to take action on a community problem, it is helpful to remember that older people
   A. are more self-reliant in their decision-making than other members of the same family
   B. often need more time to decide than younger people
   C. are more likely than younger people to view community problems self-referentially
   D. tend to take a pragmatic, rather than philosophical, view of life

3.____

4. The method of group or community decision-making that is normally MOST time-consuming is
   A. majority opinion   B. consensus
   C. expert opinion   D. authority rule

4.____

5. A local adult protective services agency has identified one of the goals of its recent public outreach campaign to be the mobilization of activists.
The campaign should probably
   A. target neutral audiences
   B. home in on supporters
   C. stick to purely factual information
   D. try to persuade community fence-sitters

5.____

6. Research of Native American youths' perceptions of family concerns for their well-being has generally found that these youths
   A. have a high degree of uncertainty about their families' feelings toward them
   B. believe their families don't care about them
   C. believe that their mothers care a great deal about them, but their fathers don't
   D. believe their families care a great deal about them

7. A domestic violence specialist is developing a new outreach program for the local community. The specialist has defined the target problem, set program goals, and planned the actions that will take place as a result of the program. Most likely, the next step will be to
   A. evaluate the resources available to achieve program goals
   B. define and sequence the steps that will be taken to achieve program goals
   C. determine how the program will be evaluated
   D. decide how the program will operate

8. Elder: *I'm so glad to have someone to talk to, someone who really understands my problem.*
   Specialist: *It is nice to be able to talk to someone who will listen.*
   Elder: *That's for sure.*
   In the above exchange, what listening skill is evident in the underlined statement?
   A. Verbatim response
   B. Paraphrasing
   C. Advising
   D. Evaluation

9. Which of the following activities is involved in the specialist's task of mobilizing?
   A. Meeting individuals in the community with problems and assisting them in finding help
   B. Identifying unmet community needs
   C. Speaking out against an unjust policy or procedure
   D. Developing new services or linking presently available services to meet community needs

10. The preliminary research associated with a public outreach campaign should FIRST be aimed at determining
    A. the budget
    B. the message's ultimate audience
    C. what media to use
    D. the short-term behavioral goals of the campaign

11. A specialist in a low-income community wants to plan programs that will deal with the influence of unemployment on domestic disturbances. The specialist needs to know not only how many unemployed people are in the community now, but also how many people will be unemployed at any particular tie in the future, and how those numbers will vary given certain conditions.

Probably the BEST way to trace employment rates over time and within differing conditions is through the use of
A. the critical path
B. linear programming
C. difference equations
D. the Markov model

12. Generally, public outreach programs—whatever their stated goal—should
I. create a sense of urgency about a problem
II. decline to identify opponents of the issue or idea
III. propose concrete, easily understandable solutions
IV. urge a specific action

The CORRECT answer is:
A. I only
B. I, III and IV
C. II and III
D. I, II, III and IV

12.____

13. Which of the following methods of community needs assessment relies to the GREATEST degree on existing public records?
A. Social indicators
B. Field study
C. Rates under treatment
D. Key informant

13.____

14. During an interview with a Native American client, a specialist is careful to maintain close and nearly constant eye contact.
The client is MOST likely to interpret this as a(n)
A. show of high concern
B. sign of disrespect
C. uncomfortable assumption of intimacy
D. attempt to intimidate

14.____

15. The BEST strategy for addressing an audience that is known to be captive, or even hostile, is to
A. refer to experiences in common
B. flatter the audience
C. joke about things in or near the audience
D. plead for fairness

15.____

16. Integrative conflict resolution is characterized by
A. an overriding concern to maximize joint outcomes
B. one side's interests opposing the other's
C. a fixed and limited amount of resources to be divided, so that the more one group gets, the less another gets
D. manipulation and withholding information as negotiation strategies

16.____

17. A specialist wants to learn how to interact with the members of a largely Latino community in a more culturally sensitive way.
Which of the following is NOT a guideline for interacting with members of a Latino community?
A. Efforts to foster independence and self-reliance may be interpreted by many Latinos as a lack of concern for others.
B. Efforts to deal one-on-one with an adolescent client may serve to alienate the parents, especially the mother.

17.____

C. A nonverbal gesture, such as lowering the eyes, is interpreted by many Latinos as a sign of respect and deference to authority.
D. In much of Latino culture, the focus of control for problems tends to be much more external than internal.

18. Each of the following is a supporting assumption of community organization, EXCEPT:
    A. Democracy requires cooperative participation.
    B. In order for communities to change, it is necessary for each individual in the community to be willing to change.
    C. Communities often need help with organization and planning.
    D. Holistic approaches work better than fragmented or ad-hoc programs.

19. Helping professionals often have difficulty to bring community resources together to fulfill unmet community needs.
    Which of the following is NOT usually a reason for this?
    A. Some community groups resist assistance when it is offered.
    B. Few community groups make their needs known.
    C. Community resources frequently change the type of services they offer.
    D. Often, community resources prefer to work alone.

20. When dealing with groups or populations of elderly clients, specialists should be mindful that about _____ of the nation's elderly suffer from mental health problems.
    A. a tenth   B. a quarter   C. a third   D. half

21. In an African-American community, a specialist from another culture should recognize that church participation, for most African-Americans, is viewed as a
    A. method for maintaining control and communicating competency
    B. way of depersonalizing problems or troubles
    C. way to divert attention away from problems
    D. means of cathartic emotional release

22. Adult protective service programs supported by state statutes protect elderly people from abuse and neglect under the doctrine of
    A. parens patriae   B. habeas corpus
    C. in loco parentis   D. volenti non fit injuria

23. In terms of public outreach, which of the following statements about an audience is NOT generally true?
    A. The more heterogeneous the audience, the more necessary it will be to use specific examples and appeals to certain types of people.
    B. The smaller the audience, the more likely that its members will share assumptions and values.
    C. When the speaker does not know the status of an audience, it is best to assume that they are captive rather than voluntary.
    D. The larger an audience, the more formal a presentation is likely to be.

24. A specialist often spends time in the places frequented by community residents. She listens carefully to what residents seem most concerned about, and engages many in conversations, asking them how they see the problems in the community. During these conversations, she makes mental notes about whether the statements of the problems are the same things that are mentioned in their conversations. From these conversations, the worker determines what she thinks the unmet needs of the community are.
Which of the key issues in identifying unmet needs has the worker neglected to address?
    A. The different points of view regarding the issues, and whether there is any common ground
    B. Whether the stated problems and conversations with community residents reflect the same concerns
    C. How community residents define the issues
    D. What the residents talk about with one another in a community

24._____

25. Which of the following political styles should be used to promote an issue that could become controversial if it is perceived to involve major reforms?
    A. High-conflict, polarized
    B. High-conflict, consensual
    C. Moderate conflict, compromise-oriented
    D. Low-conflict, technical

25._____

KEY (CORRECT ANSWERS)

1.	C	11.	D
2.	A	12.	B
3.	B	13.	A
4.	B	14.	B
5.	B	15.	A
6.	D	16.	A
7.	A	17.	D
8.	B	18.	B
9.	D	19.	C
10.	B	20.	B

21.	D
22.	A
23.	A
24.	A
25.	D

EXAMINATION SECTION
TEST 1

DIRECTIONS: Each question or incomplete statement is followed by several suggested answers or completions. Select the one that BEST answers the question or completes the statement. *PRINT THE LETTER OF THE CORRECT ANSWER IN THE SPACE AT THE RIGHT.*

1. A group member who starts out at the same level as other group members and is able to move into a leadership position within that group would be described as what kind of a leader?
   A. Autocratic   B. Democratic   C. Emergent   D. Informal

   1.____

2. Your boss is only effective as the leader of your department when you and your coworkers are motivated experts on the topic at hand. If any of you do not really have expertise in a given field, his leadership falters somewhat. What type of leader is your boss?
   A. Laissez-faire   B. Technical   C. Democratic   D. Autocratic

   2.____

3. If a leader is in charge of an inexperienced group that does not have the appropriate information and proficiency to successfully complete a task, which of the following approaches should the leader use in order for success to follow within the group?
   A. Yelling   B. Delegating   C. Participating   D. Selling

   3.____

4. If you are a democratic leader, which of the following styles will be reflective of your leadership technique?
   A. Participating   B. Telling   C. Yelling   D. Delegating

   4.____

5. In producing equality in group member participation, which of the following should a leader NOT do?
   A. Make a statement or ask a question after each person in the group has said something
   B. Avoid taking a position during disagreements
   C. Limit comments to specific individuals within the group
   D. Control dominating speakers

   5.____

6. Social capital is BEST defined as
   A. social connections that help us make more money
   B. social connections that improve our lives
   C. a type of connection that experts believe is becoming more common in Europe than the United States.
   D. none of the above

   6.____

7. Communication is not simply sending a message. It is creating true
   A. connectivity   B. understanding
   C. empathy   D. power

   7.____

8. Of the following, which is NOT a part of the speech communication process? 8.____
   A. Feedback B. Central idea
   C. Interference D. Ethics

9. You are leading a meeting and afterwards your colleagues tell you they didn't 9.____
   quite understand what you were communicating verbally and nonverbally to
   them. Which part of the communication process do you need to work on?
   A. Channel B. Main idea
   C. Message D. Specific purpose

10. If nonverbal messages contradict verbal symbols, you are sending what 10.____
    kind of message to your public?
    A. Clear B. Mixed
    C. Controversial D. Negative

11. Which of the following would a public speaker use to deliver verbal symbols? 11.____
    A. Words B. Gestures
    C. Tone D. Facial expression

12. You are in the process of taking a course on interacting with the public. Your 12.____
    instructor starts talking about "the pathway" used to transmit a message. He
    explains that "the pathway" is better known as a
    A. link B. loop C. transmitter D. channel

13. You finish an informational meeting with members of a community 13.____
    concerning a new park that will be built nearby. Afterwards, you are seeking
    feedback from them. Which of the following would NOT be a form of helpful
    feedback to you?
    A. Listeners raise their hands to point out a mistake
    B. Videotape the presentation
    C. Have colleagues and/or friends critique your presentation
    D. Hand out evaluation forms to listeners and have them fill it out after the
       presentation

14. Many public speaking experts have often repeated the famous quote, "A yawn 14.____
    is a silent _____," which references the quality of engagement within a
    presentation.
    A. rudeness B. insult C. shout D. protest

15. If a child is running around during your speech and making a lot of noise, 15.____
    what type of interference would that be?
    A. Situational B. External C. Internal D. Intentional

16. According to multiple recent surveys, of the five biggest mistakes that 16.____
    speakers make during a presentation, which one is the WORST?
    A. Being poorly prepared
    B. Trying to cover too much in one speech
    C. Failing to tailor a speech to the needs and interests of the audience
    D. Being boring

17. One of your colleagues has been asked to lead a meeting, and she confides 17.____
in you that she suffers from excessive stage fright. Which of the following
areas should you advise her to focus on to prevent her fear?
   A. Preparation   B. Self-confidence
   C. Experience   D. Sense of humor

18. When interacting with the public, which of the following elements should you 18.____
NEVER imagine before engaging in public speaking?
   A. Effective delivery   B. Nervousness
   C. Possibility of failure   D. Success

19. A spokesperson is giving a speech to community members and you are evaluating 19.____
him. You notice he tends to focus too much on himself and not enough on his
audience. What is one piece of advice you can give him so he can shift his
focus more to his audience?
   A. Change his amount of eye contact   B. Work on facial expressions
   C. Alter his style of speaking   D. All of the above

20. Most experts agree that the best way to eliminate excess energy would be 20.____
to do all of the following EXCEPT
   A. using visual aids
   B. gripping the lectern
   C. walking to the right and left occasionally
   D. making gestures

21. A woman has lived in Newville her whole life. Recently, the Newville 21.____
public works department made a policy change that angered her since it
completely rearranged her schedule. She calls you on the phone and displays
her displeasure with your department's recent policy change. What is the
FIRST response you should have toward her?
   A. Interrupt her to say you cannot discuss the situation until she calms down
   B. Apologize to her that she has been negatively affected by the public
      works department
   C. Listen to her and demonstrate comprehension of her situation and why
      she was upset by your department's action
   D. Give her a detailed explanation of the reasons for the policy change

22. Which of the following is generally TRUE regarding public opinion? 22.____
   A. It is hard to move people toward a strong opinion on anything
   B. It is easy to move people toward a strong opinion on anything
   C. Most public relations are devoted to repairing negative public opinion
      about individuals
   D. It is easier than previously thought to move people away from an opinion
      they hold

23. Influencing a community member's attitude really comes down to which of the 23.____
following?
   A. Journalism   B. Public relations
   C. Social psychology   D. Social action groups

24. If you attend a town hall meeting in which community members will bring up issues that require you to explain why your organization made the decisions it made, you will need to persuade them using evidence that is virtually indisputable. Which type of evidence should you stick to when explaining answers to the public?

    A. Facts
    B. Personal experience
    C. Emotions
    D. Using what appeals to the target public

    24._____

25. In the last decade, especially after all the organizational and governmental scandals, public institutions must do which of the following in order to be successful?

    A. Work hard to earn and sustain favorable public opinion
    B. Trust the instincts expressed by the general public
    C. Be cognizant of the media's power
    D. Place the needs of the executives ahead of the needs of the public and other constituents

    25._____

KEY (CORRECT ANSWERS)

1.	C	11.	A
2.	A	12.	D
3.	B	13.	A
4.	D	14.	C
5.	A	15.	B
6.	B	16.	C
7.	B	17.	A
8.	D	18.	B
9.	C	19.	D
10.	B	20.	B

21.	C
22.	D
23.	B
24.	A
25.	A

TEST 2

DIRECTIONS: Each question or incomplete statement is followed by several suggested answers or completions. Select the one that BEST answers the question or completes the statement. *PRINT THE LETTER OF THE CORRECT ANSWER IN THE SPACE AT THE RIGHT.*

1. Unique attributes of the Internet that people can enjoy include all of the following EXCEPT   1.____
   A. immediacy
   B. low cost
   C. pervasiveness
   D. value for building one-to-one human relationships

2. Which of the following is a reason that social media can be more effective than traditional means of advertising and communication?   2.____
   A. When someone mentions your brand in social media, there is much more potential for other people to notice
   B. It is easier to decipher tone and purpose through Twitter or Facebook than through personal communication
   C. Most of the people who would be interested in your brand or service are comfortable and familiar with using social media
   D. Almost anyone can step into a media relations role if primarily using social media, because it is easy to communicate effectively through social media platforms

3. You are tasked with building publicity for the upcoming reveal of a new art installation in the town you work in. Your boss tells you to contact journalists, reporters and bloggers to help spread the word. Which of the following would be the MOST effective way of getting the media to help build coverage?   3.____
   A. Send out a mass e-mail to any media members in the area detailing the art installation and why you need coverage for it
   B. Call each media outlet and find out who would most likely cover and build publicity for your project. Then reach out to them either face-to-face or through a phone call
   C. Using Twitter, tweet at the media members and introduce yourself and your art installation and ask them to help spread the word
   D. None of the above

4. When using written communication, which of the following is a MAJOR challenge of writing to listeners?   4.____
   A. Providing lots of statistics
   B. Grabbing the attention of the listener quickly
   C. Providing information that is easily reviewed
   D. Presenting lots of incidentals

5. In order to communicate well in writing, which of the following pieces of advice sounds good but doesn't actually help you?
   A. Write material for all audiences rather than focusing on one
   B. Think before writing
   C. Write simply and with clarity
   D. Write and rewrite until you have a polished, finished product

5.____

6. You send out a public newsletter that details a project that your team is currently working on. One week later, an employee on your team tells you she has received multiple phone calls from confused constituents claiming that the newsletter's readability was low. When you send out a corrected newsletter, you need to make sure that your communication is easy to
   A. read B. hear C. edit D. comprehend

6.____

7. You work for a biomedical company as a public outreach advocate. One day, an exciting e-mail circulates internally that states one of your scientists has discovered a cure for leukemia and your supervisor tasks you with writing the release. When writing the release, the newsworthy element inherent in the story is
   A. oddity B. conflict C. impact D. proximity

7.____

8. When communicating with the public through the Internet, news releases
   A. should not be sent via e-mail   B. should be succinct
   C. should be sent via "snail mail"   D. none of the above

8.____

9. What is the MAJOR advantage of organizational publications? Their ability to
   A. give sponsoring organizations a means of uncontrolled communications
   B. deliver specific, detailed information to narrowly defined target publics
   C. avoid the problems typically associated with two-way media
   D. provide a revenue source for sponsoring organizations

9.____

10. You are confronted by a question from a reporter that you do not know the answer to. What should you do?
    A. Give them other information you are certain is right
    B. Tell them that information is "off the record" and will be distributed later
    C. Say "no comment" rather than look like you're uninformed
    D. Admit that you don't know but promise to provide the information later

10.____

11. Often times, an organization will run situation analysis before they share information with the public. Which one of these "internal factors" is usually associated with a situational analysis?
    A. A communication audit   B. Community focus groups
    C. A list of media contacts   D. Strategy suggestions

11.____

12. When you are hired, your first task is to start a process of identifying who are involved and affected by a situation central to your organization. This process is MOST commonly referred to as a(n)
    A. situation interview
    B. communication audit
    C. exploratory survey
    D. stakeholder analysis

13. Once a public outreach plan is in the summative evaluation phase, which of the following is generally associated with it?
    A. Impact
    B. Implementation
    C. Attitude change
    D. Preparation

14. Which of the following Internet-related challenges is MOST significant in the public relations field?
    A. Finding stable, cost-effective internet provides
    B. Representing clients using new social media environments
    C. Staying abreast of changing technology
    D. Training staff to use social media

15. Which of the following BEST defines a public issue? Any
    A. problem that brings a public lawsuit
    B. concern that is of mutual distress to competitors
    C. issue that is of mutual concern to an organization and its stakeholders
    D. problem that is not a concern to an organization and/or one of its stakeholders

16. A handful of people are posting misleading and/or negative information about your organization. What is the MOST proactive approach to handling this situation?
    A. Buy up enough shares in the site where the negative posts are, and prevent those users from posting again
    B. Post anonymous comments on the sites to help combat the negativity
    C. Prepare news releases that discredit the inaccuracies
    D. Make policy changes to address complaints highlighted on the sites

17. Your supervisor has recently asked you to review present and future realities for interacting with the public. Why is it important to continually review these?
    A. It helps develop your vision statement
    B. It helps interpret trends for management
    C. It helps construe the organization's business plan
    D. To know what path the company should pursue

18. You are the community relations director for the public water utility plant that has been the focus of a group of activists who are opposed to the addition of fluoride to drinking water. These objectors are not only at the plant each day, but they are also very active on social media inciting negativity towards the practice. As the director of the plant, you have overwhelming evidence that contradicts what the protestors are arguing. You want to combat their social media with your own internet plan. Which of the following is the MOST appropriate action for you to take?
    A. Use utility employees to write the blog, posing as healthcare professionals
    B. Reach out to medical professionals to volunteer to tweet and message community members under their own identities, but with no reference to the utility company
    C. Write a blog yourself, identifying yourself as an employee, and quote the scientific opinions of a variety of sources
    D. Pay for medical professionals to respond through the internet, identifying the utility as their sponsor, but without disclosing the compensation

18.____

19. You have recently completed an advertising campaign to help assuage the anger of the community at changes in the upcoming summer program for the city. Which of the following measurements would be MOST effective for evaluating the campaign's impact on audience attitude?
    A. A content analysis of media coverage
    B. Studying blog postings about the issue
    C. Analyzing pre- and post-numbers of people signed up for the summer programs
    D. Conducting a pre- and post-analysis of public opinions

19.____

20. In order to measure how policy changes will affect the public, you recommend that your supervisors first run a focus group for research. They like the idea, but want you to be in charge of running the group. Which of the following should you keep in mind as you form the focus group?
    A. Participants need to be randomly selected
    B. Make sure participants are radically different from one another so you get a range of opinions
    C. Include at least seven or more people in the group. Otherwise, the sample is too small to draw any conclusions.
    D. Formulate a research plan and use it as a script so you can make sure the results are ones that will work for you and your supervisors

20.____

21. The public university has recently come under fire for not offering enough tuition savings options for students. You have been hired to help promote the programs they offer including new savings programs. What is the MOST appropriate first step for you to take?
    A. Research pricing and development costs for the services
    B. Develop a survey to discover which factors impact families' savings
    C. Conduct a situation analysis to gain better understanding of the issues
    D. Hold a focus group to determine which messages would be most effective for your program

21.____

5 (#2)

22. After receiving feedback from the public on a new program, you are concerned the results have been tainted by courtesy bias. You plan on sending out a new questionnaire, but you need to make sure the bias is discouraged in it. Which of the following techniques will be MOST effective at decreasing the partiality?
    A. Make questionnaire responses confidential
    B. Employ an outside firm to run the survey
    C. Offer a larger range of responses in the survey
    D. Both "A" and "C"

22.____

23. You have just relocated from Omaha, Nebraska to a branch in Chicago, Illinois. In order to communicate well while in Chicago, you must remember that
    A. most publics have the same needs
    B. all publics are most interested only in technology you are using
    C. each audience has its own special needs and require different types of communication
    D. all audiences' needs overlap

23.____

24. Recently, the Parks and Recreation Department has come under fire because it has been accused of too much marketing and not enough public relations. Which of the following, if true, would lend credibility to these accusations?
    A. Employees are focused on signing citizens up for as many different camps and activities available over the summer as possible
    B. Management consistently tries to send appreciation gifts to members of the community when they have volunteered or attending an activity sponsored by the Park district
    C. Weekly meetings are held to determine how to best improve the Park district's image as it relates to consumers
    D. Parks and Recreation is primarily focused on making sure the public enjoys their activities and trusts them to put on educational programs for the children

24.____

25. During your speech, a community member stands up and accuses you of "spinning" a story. Which of the following BEST describes their accusation?
    A. You are relating a message through an agreed-upon ethical practice within the public relations community
    B. You are twisting a message to create performance where there is none
    C. You are trying to preserve hard-earned credibility
    D. You are providing the media with balanced and accurate information

25.____

KEY (CORRECT ANSWERS)

1. D
2. A
3. C
4. B
5. D

6. D
7. C
8. B
9. B
10. D

11. A
12. D
13. A
14. C
15. C

16. B
17. A
18. C
19. D
20. A

21. C
22. D
23. C
24. A
25. B

TEST 3

DIRECTIONS: Each question or incomplete statement is followed by several suggested answers or completions. Select the one that BEST answers the question or completes the statement. *PRINT THE LETTER OF THE CORRECT ANSWER IN THE SPACE AT THE RIGHT.*

1. In order to be successful in relating to the public, all of the following are vital EXCEPT
    A. performance
    B. relationship building
    C. formal education
    D. diversity of experience

    1.____

2. Which of the following is TRUE of communicating well regarding public relations experts?
    A. It will differentiate you and your role from others with special skills in the organization you work for
    B. It should be handled delicately in order to avoid upsetting stakeholders
    C. It is not as important as looking fashionable
    D. It is less important than understanding bureaucratic peculiarities

    2.____

3. You are critiquing a staffer who will lead an important meeting in two days and you note that she keeps using words that are steeped with connotation. You tell her to be careful of these words. Why?
    A. They transmit meaning too clearly, and you always want to leave wiggle room in your meaning
    B. They transmit the dictionary definition of a word that makes for a boring presentation
    C. They transmit meaning with an emotional overtone that could lead to misunderstanding in an overall message
    D. They lend themselves to stereotyping

    3.____

4. If you are trying to avoid biasing your intended audience, which of the following factors could help with that?
    A. Symbols
    B. Objective reporting by media
    C. Semantics
    D. Peers

    4.____

5. Of the following, which trait is MOST desirable when working with the public?
    A. Having the "gift for gab"
    B. Being an elite strategist
    C. Being able to leap organizational boundaries
    D. Performing well, especially in crises

    5.____

6. Which of the following areas is likely to see continual growth in the practice of public relations?
    A. Healthcare
    B. Social media
    C. Law enforcement
    D. None of the above

    6.____

7. What is the MOST commonly used public relations tactic?
   A. A news release
   B. A special event
   C. A PSA (public service announcement)
   D. A full feature news article

7.____

8. You have just been assigned to help with a new advertising campaign that will promote the new services offered by your organization. One major component of the new campaign will focus on publicity through photographs. Knowing you need to get this part of the project right, which of the following is the BEST tip to remember when taking PR photos?
   A. Don't use action shots because they usually wind up blurry
   B. Make sure there is good contrast and sharp detail
   C. Ensure that the product/services are the biggest thing(s) in the photo
   D. Photograph multiple people rather than only one

8.____

9. Which of the following situations would merit holding a press conference?
   A. When a corporation is restructured
   B. When a new public relations employee has been hired
   C. When information is of minor relevance to a specific audience
   D. When there is a new product to be released

9.____

10. On average, how long should an announcement to the public last on the radio?
    A. 2 minutes   B. 20 seconds   C. 1 minute   D. 10 seconds

10.____

11. In educating the public, you need to develop a PR plan and analyze each situation that could arise. Which of the following should NOT be a part of the analysis?
    A. Research   B. Message crafting
    C. Creating a problem statement   D. Asking the 5 W's and the H

11.____

12. You are in charge of promoting an event in the near future, but social media is unavailable to you at this time. Which of the following is the BEST way to get your message out to the media and, therefore, the public?
    A. An Op-Ed piece in the local newspaper
    B. A press conference
    C. A newsletter
    D. A news release

12.____

13. In the past few months, you and your colleagues have been accused of "doublespeak". Which of the following excerpts from presentations you have used could you defend and explain why it would NOT be an example of "doublespeak"?
    A. You called combat "fighting"
    B. Fred referred to genocide as "ethnic cleansing"
    C. Your boss referred to recent layoffs as "downsizing"
    D. Susie called the janitor a "custodial engineer"

13.____

14. In relating to the public, which of the following reflects key words in defining modern day PR?
    A. Deliberate, public interest, management function
    B. Persuasive, manipulative, improvisation
    C. Management, technical, flexible
    D. Influential, creative, evaluative

15. How is educating and relating to the public different from being a journalist, marketing agent, or advertiser?
    A. It is more focused on advocacy
    B. It is about getting "free" press coverage
    C. It is about building relationships with various demographics
    D. All of the above

16. Of the following, what is the BEST tactic for learning employee attitudes?
    A. Internal communications audit
    B. Research
    C. Conference meeting
    D. Both A and B

17. When releasing news to the public, you should make sure it reads at a _____-grade reading level.
    A. 5th   B. 12th   C. 9th   D. 7th

18. If you are using a euphemism that actually changes the meaning/impact of a concept you are trying to relay, what is that called?
    A. Insider language
    B. Doublespeak
    C. Stylizing
    D. Plagiarism

19. Which of the following should be included in a public relations campaign if you want to ensure people will hear, understand, and believe your message?
    A. Repetition
    B. Imagery
    C. Thoroughness
    D. Acceptance

20. In PR, what is it called when you track coverage and compare it over a period of time?
    A. Bookmarking
    B. Benchmarking
    C. Comparison analysis
    D. Correspondence

21. What is a baseline study PRIMARILY used for?
    A. To determine changes in audience perception and attitude
    B. To figure out how well your company is doing in the marketplace compared to your competitors
    C. To find out the cost of buying space taken up by a particular article if that article is an advertisement
    D. None of the above

22. Of the following people, who would BEST be considered a modern role model for successful public relations?
    A. Phineas T. Barnum (Barnum and Bailey)
    B. Ivy Lee
    C. Andrew Jackson
    D. Sir Walter Raleigh

23. If your organization has recently participated in a "publicity stunt," what type of PR strategy have you just used?
    A. Community
    B. Lobbying
    C. News management
    D. Crisis management

24. You tell your supervisor that you want to start using video press releases. When he presses you to explain why, you tell him that you want to take advantage of the fact that
    A. many news agencies don't review them ahead of broadcasting
    B. most reporters hired to create them have contacts within the industry
    C. they cover stories that some local news organizations cannot
    D. the production value may be better than those at local stations

25. A _____ is a type of news leak in which the source reveals large policy changes are on the table.
    A. disclosure
    B. hook
    C. exclusive
    D. trial balloon

KEY (CORRECT ANSWERS)

1. C
2. B
3. C
4. B
5. D

6. B
7. A
8. B
9. D
10. C

11. B
12. D
13. A
14. A
15. D

16. D
17. C
18. B
19. A
20. B

21. A
22. B
23. C
24. C
25. D

TEST 4

DIRECTIONS: Each question or incomplete statement is followed by several suggested answers or completions. Select the one that BEST answers the question or completes the statement. *PRINT THE LETTER OF THE CORRECT ANSWER IN THE SPACE AT THE RIGHT.*

1. The Facial Feedback Hypothesis is a popular nonverbal theory that is BEST defined as
   A. people mirroring each other's facial expressions
   B. emotions leading to certain facial expressions
   C. facial expression can lead to the experience of certain emotions
   D. looking into a mirror while making a facial expression can cause one to change their facial expression

   1.____

2. Of the following, which is NOT recognized as a function of smiling?
   A. It provides feedback.
   B. It signals disinterest.
   C. It helps establish rapport.
   D. It signals attentiveness.

   2.____

3. When facial expressions are limited by cultural expectations, that is referred to as
   A. display rules
   B. syntactic displays
   C. adaptors
   D. interaction intensification

   3.____

4. Of the following, which is recognized as part of the six basic emotions across cultures globally?
   A. Guilt
   B. Happiness
   C. Fear
   D. Both B and C

   4.____

5. Which kinds of communication scenarios are more likely to see leadership roles develop from?
   A. Small group
   B. Intrapersonal communication
   C. Face-to-face public communication
   D. Text messaging

   5.____

6. Which of the following highlights the key difference between small group communication and organizational communication?
   A. Feedback is easier and more immediate in organizational.
   B. Communication is more informal in small group communication.
   C. The message is easier to adapt to the specific needs of the receiver in organizational communication.
   D. People are more spread out in small group communication.

   6.____

7. Which of the following would be an example of mediated communication?
   A. A principal addresses the student body in a speech.
   B. Two friends communicate while they work together in class.
   C. An employee texts his coworkers to see if they want to hang out after work.
   D. Three friends joke with one another while attending a concert.

   7.____

8. Which of the following is FALSE concerning the way interpersonal relationships can affect us physically?
   A. Without interpersonal relationships, we can become sick
   B. These interpersonal relationships are necessary for humans; according to most research, humans raised in isolation are less healthy than those raised with others
   C. Humans are not the only mammals that need relationships in order to survive and thrive
   D. Interpersonal relationships are necessary until about age 12, but not later in adulthood

9. Which of the following is a characteristic of public relationships as they compare to private relationships?
   A. Intrinsic rewards
   B. Normative rules
   C. Use of particularistic knowledge
   D. Small number of intimates

10. When someone asks how you know they were angry, it is likely they fall into which style of facial expressions?
    A. Withholder
    B. Revealer
    C. Frozen-affect expressor
    D. Unwitting expressor

11. The theory of expectancy violations is BEST defined as
    A. nonverbal behavior reciprocated based primarily on positive or negative valence and the perceived reward value of the other person
    B. the process of intimacy exchange within a dyad relationship
    C. a social rule that says we should repay in kind what another has provided us
    D. none of the above

12. If an employee has a very good idea of what is and is not socially acceptable in any given situation, which kind of linguistic competence is she strong in?
    A. Phonemic   B. Syntactic   C. Pragmatic   D. Semantic

13. Which of the following would NOT be considered sexist language?
    A. Although a girl, Sonia is very brave.
    B. A gorgeous model, Johnny also likes to use his surfboard on the weekends.
    C. Jimmy's brother is a male nurse.
    D. None; all are considered to be sexist.

14. What is it called when individual experience, and NOT conventional agreement, creates meaning?
    A. Small talk communication
    B. Denotative meaning
    C. Connotative meaning
    D. Self-reflexive communication

15. Which of the following kinds of communication do students spend the MOST time engaged in?
    A. Listening   B. Writing   C. Reading   D. Speaking

16. Which of the following would be evidence of active listening?
    A. Maintain eye contact
    B. Nodding and making eye contact
    C. Asking for clarification
    D. All of the above

    16.____

17. When listening in an evaluative context, which of the following must be done for it to be considered successful?
    A. Precisely disseminate stimuli in a message
    B. Comprehend the intended meaning of a message
    C. Make critical assessments of the accuracy of the facts in a message
    D. All of the above

    17.____

18. A friend visits one day and tells you she thinks her husband is cheating on her with his ex-wife. She tells you she doesn't know what to do because she can't imagine living without him. If you wanted to paraphrase, which of the following BEST exemplifies that?
    A. "You are feeling insecure because you don't have a very good relationship with your husband."
    B. "You're afraid your husband is seeing his ex-wife behind your back; you don't know what to do; and you can't live without him."
    C. "You're afraid that your husband may still have feelings for his ex-wife and you're afraid you'll lose him."
    D. "Don't worry; his ex-wife is not back with him. You're just being paranoid."

    18.____

19. When we form impressions of others, when might the recency effect impact our assessments? If we
    A. focus on our own feelings instead of the feelings of others
    B. are motivated to be more accurate or expect to be held accountable for our own perceptions
    C. engage in self-monitoring of our behaviors
    D. employ the discounting rule

    19.____

20. Which of the following BEST defines a "modal self"?
    A. The ideal person for a social order
    B. A person who does not go to extremes
    C. The kind of self valued in the 20th century but not the 21st century
    D. The person who monitors his own behavior in social situations

    20.____

21. Which of the following is TRUE of today's society?
    A. People are less selfish than they have ever been.
    B. People spend most of their time trying to be a single, unitary self.
    C. People have many short-lived relationships leading to their notions of themselves changing easily.
    D. People try to be frugal, honorable, and self-sacrificing.

    21.____

22. A man's childhood consisted of a dismissing attachment style. Which of the following behaviors will he MOST likely exhibit as an adult?
    A. Anxiousness and ambivalence
    B. Obsessive friendliness and dependence
    C. Autonomy and distance from others
    D. Rhetorical sensitivity

23. When practicing self-disclosure, which of the following is a good rule of thumb?
    A. Be sure to disclose more than your partner
    B. Reserve your most important disclosures for people you know well
    C. Ignore the style of disclosure; the only thing that is important is content
    D. All of the above

24. During your first meeting as project leader, you approach your group and inform them that John will serve as your assistant project leader. He will be responsible for chairing team meetings and establishing the agenda. When John is given this formal leadership position, what type of power does he have over the other members of the project?
    A. Legitimate   B. Reward   C. Expert   D. Punishment

25. If you bring an employee to lead a project because she is knowledgeable and skilled in the area the project focuses on, what type of power does she possess?
    A. Legitimate   B. Reward   C. Referent   D. Expert

KEY (CORRECT ANSWERS)

1.	C		11.	A
2.	B		12.	C
3.	A		13.	D
4.	D		14.	C
5.	A		15.	A
6.	B		16.	D
7.	C		17.	C
8.	D		18.	B
9.	B		19.	D
10.	D		20.	A

21. C
22. C
23. B
24. A
25. D

COMMUNICATION

EXAMINATION SECTION
TEST 1

DIRECTIONS: Each question or incomplete statement is followed by several suggested answers or completions. Select the one that BEST answers the question or completes the statement. *PRINT THE LETTER OF THE CORRECT ANSWER IN THE SPACE AT THE RIGHT.*

1. In some agencies the counsel to the agency head is given the right to bypass the chain of command and issue orders directly to the staff concerning matters that involve certain specific processes and practices.
   This situation MOST nearly illustrates the principle of _____ authority.
   A. the acceptance theory of
   B. multiple-linear
   C. splintered
   D. functional

   1._____

2. It is commonly understood that communication is an important part of the administrative process.
   Which of the following is NOT a valid principle of the communication process in administration?
   A. The channels of communication should be spontaneous.
   B. The lines of communication should be as direct and as short as possible.
   C. Communications should be authenticated.
   D. The persons serving in communications centers should be competent.

   2._____

3. Of the following, the one factor which is generally considered LEAST essential to successful committee operations is
   A. stating a clear definition of the authority and scope of the committee
   B. selecting the committee chairman carefully
   C. limiting the size of the committee to four persons
   D. limiting the subject matter to that which can be handled in group discussion

   3._____

4. Of the following, the failure by line managers to accept and appreciate the benefits and limitations of a new program or system VERY FREQUENTLY can be traced to the
   A. budgetary problems involved
   B. resultant need to reduce staff
   C. lack of controls it engenders
   D. failure of top management to support its implementation

   4._____

5. If a manager were thinking about using a committee of subordinates to solve an operating problem, which of the following would generally NOT be an advantage of such use of the committee approach?
   A. Improved coordination
   B. Low cost
   C. Increased motivation
   D. Integrated judgment

   5._____

41

6. Every supervisor has many occasions to lead a conference or participate in a conference of some sort.
Of the following statements that pertain to conferences and conference leadership, which is generally considered to be MOST valid?
   A. Since World War II, the trend has been toward fewer shared decisions and more conferences.
   B. The most important part of a conference leader's job is to direct discussion.
   C. In providing opportunities for group interaction, management should avoid consideration of its past management philosophy.
   D. A good administrator cannot lead a good conference if he is a poor public speaker.

7. Of the following, it is usually LEAST desirable for a conference leader to
   A. call the name of a person after asking a question
   B. summarize proceedings periodically
   C. make a practice of repeating questions
   D. ask a question without indicating who is to reply

8. Assume that, in a certain organization, a situation has developed in which there is little difference in status or authority between individuals.
Which of the following would be the MOST likely result with regard to communication in this organization?
   A. Both the accuracy and flow of communication will be improved.
   B. Both the accuracy and flow of communication will substantially decrease.
   C. Employees will seek more formal lines of communication.
   D. Neither the flow nor the accuracy of communication will be improved over the former hierarchical structure.

9. The main function of many agency administrative officers is "information management." Information that is received by an administrative officer may be classified as active or passive, depending upon whether or not it requires the recipient to take some action.
Of the following, the item received which is clearly the MOST active information is
   A. an appointment of a new staff member
   B. a payment voucher for a new desk
   C. a press release concerning a past event
   D. the minutes of a staff meeting

10. Of the following, the one LEAST considered to be a communication barrier is
    A. group feedback
    B. charged words
    C. selective perception
    D. symbolic meanings

11. Management studies support the hypothesis that, in spite of the tendency of employees to censor the information communicated to their supervisor, subordinates are more likely to communicate problem-oriented information UPWARD when they have a
    A. long period of service in the organization
    B. high degree of trust in the supervisor
    C. high educational level
    D. low status on the organizational ladder

11.____

12. Electronic data processing equipment can produce more information faster than can be generated by any other means.
    In view of this, the MOST important problem faced by management at present is to
    A. keep computers fully occupied
    B. find enough computer personnel
    C. assimilate and properly evaluate the information
    D. obtain funds to establish appropriate information systems

12.____

13. A well-designed management information system essentially provides each executive and manager the information he needs for
    A. determining computer time requirements
    B. planning and measuring results
    C. drawing a new organization chart
    D. developing a new office layout

13.____

14. It is generally agreed that management policies should be periodically reappraised and restated in accordance with current conditions.
    Of the following, the approach which would be MOST effective in determining whether a policy should be revised is to
    A. conduct interviews with staff members at all levels in order to ascertain the relationship between the policy and actual practice
    B. make proposed revisions in the policy and apply it to current problems
    C. make up hypothetical situations using both the old policy and a revised version in order to make comparisons
    D. call a meeting of top level staff in order to discuss ways of revising the policy

14.____

15. Your superior has asked you to notify division employees of an important change in one of the operating procedures described in the division manual. Every employee presently has a copy of this manual.
    Which of the following is normally the MOST practical way to get the employees to understand such a change?
    A. Notify each employee individually of the change and answer any questions he might have
    B. Send a written notice to key personnel, directing them to inform the people under them

15.____

C. Call a general meeting, distribute a corrected page for the manual, and discuss the change
D. Send a memo to employees describing the change in general terms and asking them to make the necessary corrections in their copies of the manual

16. Assume that the work in your department involves the use of any technical terms.
In such a situation, when you are answering inquiries from the general public, it would usually be BEST to
    A. use simple language and avoid the technical terms
    B. employ the technical terms whenever possible
    C. bandy technical terms freely, but explain each term in parentheses
    D. apologize if you are forced to use a technical term

16._____

17. Suppose that you receive a telephone call from someone identifying himself as an employee in another city department who asks to be given information which your own department regards as confidential.
Which of the following is the BEST way of handling such a request?
    A. Give the information requested, since your caller as official standing
    B. Grant the request, provided the caller gives you a signed receipt
    C. Refuse the request, because you have no way of knowing whether the caller is really who he claims to be
    D. Explain that the information is confidential and inform the caller of the channels he must go through to have the information released to him

17._____

18. Studies show that office employees place high importance on the social and human aspects of the organization. What office employees like best about their jobs is the kind of people with whom they work. So strive hard to group people who are most likely to get along well together.
Based on this information, it is MOST reasonable to assume that office workers are most pleased to work in a group which
    A. is congenial   B. has high productivity
    C. allows individual creativity   D. is unlike other groups

18._____

19. A certain supervisor does not compliment members of his staff when they come up with good ideas. He feels that coming up with good ideas is part of the job and does not merit special attention.
This supervisor's practice is
    A. *poor*, because recognition for good ideas is a good motivator
    B. *poor*, because the staff will suspect that the supervisor has no good ideas of his own
    C. *good*, because it is reasonable to assume that employees will tell their supervisor of ways to improve office practice
    D. *good*, because the other members of the staff are not made to seem inferior by comparison

19._____

20. Some employees of a department have sent an anonymous letter containing many complaints to the department head.
Of the following, what is this MOST likely to show about the department?
   A. It is probably a good place to work.
   B. Communications are probably poor.
   C. The complaints are probably unjustified.
   D. These employees are probably untrustworthy.

21. Which of the following actions would usually be MOST appropriate for a supervisor to take after receiving an instruction sheet from his superior explaining a new procedure which is to be followed?
   A. Put the instruction sheet aside temporarily until he determines what is wrong with the old procedure.
   B. Call his superior and ask whether the procedure is one he must implement immediately.
   C. Write a memorandum to the superior asking for more details.
   D. Try the new procedure and advise the superior of any problems or possible improvements.

22. Of the following, which one is considered the PRIMARY advantage of using a committee to resolved a problem in an organization?
   A. No one person will be held accountable for the decision since a group of people was involved.
   B. People with different backgrounds give attention to the problem.
   C. The decision will take considerable time so there is unlikely to be a decision that will later be regretted.
   D. One person cannot dominate the decision-making process.

23. Employees in a certain office come to their supervisor with all their complaints about the office and the work. Almost every employee has had at least one minor complaint at some time.
The situation with respect to complaints in this office may BEST be described as probably
   A. *good*; employees who complain care about their jobs and work hard
   B. *good*; grievances brought out into the open can be corrected
   C. *bad*; only serious complaints should be discussed
   D. *bad*; it indicates the staff does not have confidence in the administration

24. The administrator who allows his staff to suggest ways to do their work will usually find that
   A. this practice contributes to high productivity
   B. the administrator's ideas produce greater output
   C. clerical employees suggest inefficient work methods
   D. subordinate employees resent performing a management function

25. The MAIN purpose for a supervisor's questioning the employees at a conference he is holding is to
   A. stress those areas of information covered but not understood by the participants
   B. encourage participants to think through the problem under discussion
   C. catch those subordinates who are not paying attention
   D. permit the more knowledgeable participants to display their grasp of the problems being discussed

25.____

KEY (CORRECT ANSWERS)

1.	D	11.	B
2.	A	12.	C
3.	C	13.	B
4.	D	14.	A
5.	B	15.	C
6.	B	16.	A
7.	C	17.	D
8.	D	18.	A
9.	A	19.	A
10.	A	20.	B

21.	D
22.	B
23.	B
24.	A
25.	B

TEST 2

DIRECTIONS: Each question or incomplete statement is followed by several suggested answers or completions. Select the one that BEST answers the question or completes the statement. *PRINT THE LETTER OF THE CORRECT ANSWER IN THE SPACE AT THE RIGHT.*

1. For a superior to use *consultative supervision* with his subordinates effectively, it is ESSENTIAL that he
    A. accept the fact that his formal authority will be weakened by the procedure
    B. admit that he does not know more than all his men together and that his ideas are not always best
    C. utilize a committee system so that the procedure is orderly
    D. make sure that all subordinates are consulted so that no one feels left out

    1.____

2. The *grapevine* is an informal means of communication in an organization. The attitude of a supervisor with respect to the grapevine should be to
    A. ignore it since it deals mainly with rumors and sensational information
    B. regard it as a serious danger which should be eliminated
    C. accept it as a real line of communication which should be listened to
    D. utilize it for most purposes instead of the official line of communication

    2.____

3. The supervisor of an office that must deal with the public should realize that planning in this type of work situation
    A. is useless because he does not know how many people will request service or what service they will request
    B. must be done at a higher level but that he should be ready to implement the results of such planning
    C. is useful primarily for those activities that are not concerned with public contact
    D. is useful for all the activities of the office, including those that relate to public contact

    3.____

4. Assume that it is your job to receive incoming telephone calls. Those calls which you cannot handle yourself have to be transferred to the appropriate office.
    If you receive an outside call for an extension line which is busy, the one of the following which you should do FIRST is to
    A. interrupt the person speaking on the extension and tell him a call is waiting
    B. tell the caller the line is busy and let him know every thirty seconds whether or not it is free
    C. leave the caller on "hold" until the extension is free
    D. tell the caller the line is busy and ask him if he wishes to wait

    4.____

47

5. Your superior has subscribed to several publications directly related to your division's work, and he has asked you to see to it that the publications are circulated among the supervisory personnel in the division. There are eight supervisors involved.
The BEST method of insuring that all eight see these publications is to
   A. place the publication in the division's general reference library as soon as it arrives
   B. inform each supervisor whenever a publication arrives and remind all of them that they are responsible for reading it
   C. prepare a standard slip that can be stapled to each publication, listing the eight supervisors and saying, "Please read, initial your name, and pass along"
   D. send a memo to the eight supervisors saying that they may wish to purchase individual subscriptions in their own names if they are interested in seeing each issue

5.____

6. Your superior has telephoned a number of key officials in your agency to ask whether they can meet at a certain time next month. He has found that they can all make it, and he has asked you to confirm the meeting.
Which of the following is the BEST way to confirm such a meeting?
   A. Note the meeting on your superior's calendar.
   B. Post a notice of the meeting on the agency bulletin board.
   C. Call the officials on the day of the meeting to remind them of the meeting.
   D. Write a memo to each official involved, repeating the time and place of the meeting.

6.____

7. Assume that a new city regulation requires that certain kinds of private organizations file information forms with your department. You have been asked to write the short explanatory message that will be printed on the front cover of the pamphlet containing the forms and instructions.
Which of the following would be the MOST appropriate way of beginning this message?
   A. Get the readers' attention by emphasizing immediately that there are legal penalties for organizations that fail to file before a certain date.
   B. Briefly state the nature of the enclosed forms and the types of organizations that must file.
   C. Say that your department is very sorry to have to put organizations to such an inconvenience.
   D. Quote the entire regulation adopted by the city, even if it is quite long and is expressed din complicated legal language.

7.____

8. Suppose that you have been told to make up the vacation schedule for the 18 employees in a particular unit. In order for the unit to operate effectively, only a few employees can be on vacation at the same time.
Which of the following is the MOST advisable approach in making up the schedule?
   A. Draw up a schedule assigning vacations in alphabetical order
   B. Find out when the supervisors want to take their vacations, and randomly assign whatever periods are left to the non-supervisory personnel

8.____

C. Assign the most desirable times to employees of longest standing and the least desirable times to the newest employees
D. Have all employees state their own preference, and then work out any conflicts in consultation with the people involved

9. Assume that you have been asked to prepare job descriptions for various positions in your department.
Which of the following are the basic points that should be covered in a *job description*?
   A. General duties and responsibilities of the position, with examples of day-to-day tasks
   B. Comments on the performances of present employees
   C. Estimates of the number of openings that may be available in each category during the coming year
   D. Instructions for carrying out the specific tasks assigned to your department

10. Of the following, the biggest DISADVANTAGE in allowing a free flow of communications in an agency is that such a free flow
    A. decreases creativity
    B. increases the use of the *grapevine*
    C. lengthens the chain of command
    D. reduces the executive's power to direct the flow of information

11. A downward flow of authority in an organization is one example of _____ communication.
    A. horizontal   B. informal   C. circular   D. vertical

12. Of the following, the one that would MOST likely block effective communication is
    A. concentration only on the issues at hand
    B. lack of interest or commitment
    C. use of written reports
    D. use of charts and graphs

13. An ADVANTAGE of the *lecture* as a teaching tool is that it
    A. enables a person to present his ideas to a large number of people
    B. allows the audience to retain a maximum of the information given
    C. holds the attention of the audience for the longest time
    D. enables the audience member to easily recall the main points

14. An ADVANTAGE of the *small-group* discussion as a teaching tool is that
    A. it always focuses attention on one person as the leader
    B. it places collective responsibility on the group as a whole
    C. its members gain experience by summarizing the ideas of others
    D. each member of the group acts as a member of a team

15. The one of the following that is an ADVANTAGE of a *large-group* discussion, when compared to a small-group discussion, is that the large-group discussion
    A. moves along more quickly than a small-group discussion
    B. allows its participants to feel more at ease, and speak out more freely
    C. gives the whole group a chance to exchange ideas on a certain subject at the same occasion
    D. allows its members to feel a greater sense of personal responsibility

15.____

KEY (CORRECT ANSWERS)

1.	D	6.	D	11.	D
2.	C	7.	B	12.	B
3.	D	8.	D	13.	A
4.	D	9.	A	14.	D
5.	C	10.	D	15.	C

EXAMINATION SECTION
TEST 1

DIRECTIONS: Each question or incomplete statement is followed by several suggested answers or completions. Select the one that BEST answers the question or completes the statement. *PRINT THE LETTER OF THE CORRECT ANSWER IN THE SPACE AT THE RIGHT.*

1. In public agencies, communications should be based PRIMARILY on a
    A. two-way flow from the top down and from the bottom up, most of which should be given in writing to avoid ambiguity
    B. multi-direction flow among all levels and with outside persons
    C. rapid, internal one-way flow from the top down
    D. two-way flow of information, most of which should be given orally for purposes of clarity

    1.____

2. In some organizations, changes in policy or procedures are often communicated by word of mouth from supervisors to employees with no prior discussion or exchange of viewpoints with employees.
    This procedure often produces employee dissatisfaction CHIEFLY because
    A. information is mostly unusable since a considerable amount of time is required to transmit information
    B. lower-level supervisors tend to be excessively concerned with minor details
    C. management has failed to seek employees' advice before making changes
    D. valuable staff time is lost between decision-making and the implementation of decisions

    2.____

3. For good letter writing, you should try to visualize the person to whom you are writing, especially if you know him.
    Of the following rules, it is LEAST helpful in such visualization to think of
    A. the person's likes and dislikes, his concerns, and his needs
    B. what you would be likely to say if speaking in person
    C. what you would expect to be asked if speaking in person
    D. your official position in order to be certain that your words are proper

    3.____

4. One approach to good informal letter writing is to make letters and conversational.
    All of the following practices will usually help to do this EXCEPT:
    A. If possible, use a style which is similar to the style used when speaking
    B. Substitute phrases for single words (e.g., *at the present time* for *now*)
    C. Use contractions of words (e.g., *you're* for *you are*)
    D. Use ordinary vocabulary when possible

    4.____

5. All of the following rules will aid in producing clarity in report-writing EXCEPT:
   A. Give specific details or examples, if possible
   B. Keep related words close together in each sentence
   C. Present information in sequential order
   D. Put several thoughts or ideas in each paragraph

6. The one of the following statements about public relations which is MOST accurate is that
   A. in the long run, appearance gains better results than performance
   B. objectivity is decreased if outside public relations consultants are employed
   C. public relations is the responsibility of every employee
   D. public relations should be based on a formal publicity program

7. The form of communication which is usually considered to be MOST personally directed to the intended recipient is the
   A. brochure   B. film   C. letter   D. radio

8. In general, a document that presents an organization's views or opinions on a particular topic is MOST accurately known as a
   A. tear sheet
   B. position paper
   C. flyer
   D. journal

9. Assume that you have been asked to speak before an organization of persons who oppose a newly announced program in which you are involved. You feel tense about talking to this group.
   Which of the following rules generally would be MOST useful in gaining rapport when speaking before the audience?
   A. Impress them with your experience
   B. Stress all areas of disagreement
   C. Talk to the group as to one person
   D. Use formal grammar and language

10. An organization must have an effective public relations program since, at its best, public relations is a bridge to change.
    All of the following statements about communication and human behavior have validity EXCEPT:
    A. People are more likely to talk about controversial matters with like-minded people than with those holding other views
    B. The earlier an experience, the more powerful its effect since it influences how later experiences will be interpreted
    C. In periods of social tension, official sources gain increased believability
    D. Those who are already interested in a topic are the ones who are most open to receive new communications about it

11. An employee should be encouraged to talk easily and frankly when he is dealing with his supervisor.
    In order to encourage such free communication, it would be MOST appropriate for a supervisor to behave in a(n)
    A. sincere manner; assure the employee that you will deal with him honestly and openly
    B. official manner; you are a supervisor and must always act formally with subordinates
    C. investigative manner; you must probe and question to get to a basis of trust
    D. unemotional manner; the employee's emotions and background should play no part in your dealings with him

12. Research findings show that an increase in free communication within an agency GENERALLY results in which one of the following?
    A. Improved morale and productivity
    B. Increased promotional opportunities
    C. An increase in authority
    D. A spirit of honesty

13. Assume that you are a supervisor and your superiors have given you a new-type procedure to be followed.
    Before passing this information on to your subordinates, the one of the following actions that you should take FIRST is to
    A. ask your superiors to send out a memorandum to the entire staff
    B. clarify the procedure in your own mind
    C. set up a training course to provide instruction on the new procedure
    D. write a memorandum to your subordinates

14. Communication is necessary for an organization to be effective.
    The one of the following which is LEAST important for most communication systems is that
    A. messages are sent quickly and directly to the person who needs them to operate
    B. information should be conveyed understandably and accurately
    C. the method used to transmit information should be kept secret so that security can be maintained
    D. senders of messages must know how their messages are received and acted upon

15. Which one of the following is the CHIEF advantage of listening willingly to subordinates and encouraging them to talk freely and honestly?
    It
    A. reveals to supervisors the degree to which ideas that are passed down are accepted by subordinates
    B. reduces the participation of subordinates in the operation of the department
    C. encourages subordinates to try for promotion
    D. enables supervisors to learn more readily what the *grapevine* is saying

16. A supervisor may be informed through either oral or written reports. 16.____
    Which one of the following is an ADVANTAGE of using oral reports?
    A. There is no need for a formal record of the report.
    B. An exact duplicate of the report is not easily transmitted to others.
    C. A good oral report requires little time for preparation.
    D. An oral report involves two-way communication between a subordinate and his supervisor.

17. Of the following, the MOST important reason why supervisors should 17.____
    communicate effectively with the public is to
    A. improve the public's understanding of information that is important for them to know
    B. establish a friendly relationship
    C. obtain information about the kinds of people who come to the agency
    D. convince the public that services are adequate

18. Supervisors should generally NOT use phrases like *too hard*, *too easy*, and 18.____
    a lot PRINCIPALLY because such phrases
    A. may be offensive to some minority groups
    B. are too informal
    C. mean different things to different people
    D. are difficult to remember

19. The ability to communicate clearly and concisely is an important element in 19.____
    effective leadership.
    Which of the following statements about oral and written communication is GENERALLY true?
    A. Oral communication is more time-consuming.
    B. Written communication is more likely to be misinterpreted.
    C. Oral communication is useful only in emergencies.
    D. Written communication is useful mainly when giving information to fewer than twenty people.

20. Rumors can often have harmful and disruptive effects on an organization. 20.____
    Which one of the following is the BEST way to prevent rumors from becoming a problem?
    A. Refuse to act on rumors, thereby making them less believable.
    B. Increase the amount of information passed along by the *grapevine*.
    C. Distribute as much factual information as possible.
    D. Provide training in report writing.

21. Suppose that a subordinate asks you about a rumor he has heard. The rumor 21.____
    deals with a subject which your superiors consider *confidential*.
    Which of the following BEST describes how you should answer the subordinate? Tell

A. the subordinate that you don't make the rules and that he should speak to higher ranking officials
B. the subordinate that you will ask your superior for information
C. him only that you cannot comment on the matter
D. him the rumor is not true

22. Supervisors often find it difficult to *get their message across* when instructing newly appointed employees in their various duties.
The MAIN reason for this is generally that the
    A. duties of the employees have increased
    B. supervisor is often so expert in his area that he fails to see it from the learner's point of view
    C. supervisor adapts his instruction to the slowest learner in the group
    D. new employees are younger, less concerned with job security and more interested in fringe benefits

23. Assume that you are discussing a job problem with an employee under your supervision. During the discussion, you see that the man's eyes are turning away from you and that he is not paying attention.
In order to get the man's attention, you should FIRST
    A. ask him to look you in the eye
    B. talk to him about sports
    C. tell him he is being very rude
    D. change your tone of voice

24. As a supervisor, you may find it necessary to conduct meetings with your subordinates.
Of the following, which would be MOST helpful in assuring that a meeting accomplishes the purpose for which it was called?
    A. Give notice of the conclusions you would like to reach at the start of the meeting.
    B. Delay the start of the meeting until everyone is present.
    C. Write down points to be discussed in proper sequence.
    D. Make sure everyone is clear on whatever conclusions have been reached and on what must be done after the meeting.

25. Every supervisor will occasionally be called upon to deliver a reprimand to a subordinate. If done properly, this can greatly help an employee improve his performance.
Which one of the following is NOT a good practice to follow when giving a reprimand?
    A. Maintain your composure and temper
    B. Reprimand a subordinate in the presence of other employees so they can learn the same lesson
    C. Try to understand why the employee was not able to perform satisfactorily
    D. Let your knowledge of the man involved determine the exact nature of the reprimand

KEY (CORRECT ANSWERS)

1. C
2. B
3. D
4. B
5. D

6. C
7. C
8. B
9. C
10. C

11. A
12. A
13. B
14. C
15. A

16. D
17. A
18. C
19. B
20. C

21. B
22. B
23. D
24. D
25. B

TEST 2

DIRECTIONS: Each question or incomplete statement is followed by several suggested answers or completions. Select the one that BEST answers the question or completes the statement. *PRINT THE LETTER OF THE CORRECT ANSWER IN THE SPACE AT THE RIGHT.*

1. Usually one thinks of communication as a single step, essentially that of transmitting an idea.
   Actually, however, this is only part of a total process, the FIRST step of which should be
   A. the prompt dissemination of the idea to those who may be affected by it
   B. motivating those affected to take the required action
   C. clarifying the idea in one's own mind
   D. deciding to whom the idea is to be communicated

   1.____

2. Research studies on patterns of informal communication have concluded that most individuals in a group tend to be passive recipients of news, while a few make it their business to spread it around in an organization.
   With this conclusion in mind, it would be MOST correct for the supervisor to attempt to identify these few individuals and
   A. give them the complete facts on important matters in advance of others
   B. inform the other subordinates of the identity of these few individuals so that their influence may be minimized
   C. keep them straight on the facts on important matters
   D. warn them to cease passing along any information to others

   2.____

3. The one of the following which is the PRINCIPAL advantage of making an oral report is that it
   A. affords an immediate opportunity for two-way communication between the subordinate and superior
   B. is an easy method for the superior to use in transmitting information to others of equal rank
   C. saves the time of all concerned
   D. permits more precise pinpointing of praise or blame by means of follow-up questions by the superior

   3.____

4. An agency may sometimes undertake a public relations program of a defensive nature.
   With reference to the use of defensive public relations, it would be MOST correct to state that it
   A. is bound to be ineffective since defensive statements, even though supported by factual data, can never hope to even partly overcome the effects of prior unfavorable attacks
   B. proves that the agency has failed to establish good relationships with newspapers, radio stations, or other means of publicity

   4.____

57

C. shows that the upper echelons of the agency have failed to develop sound public relations procedures and techniques
D. is sometimes required to aid morale by protecting the agency from unjustified criticism and misunderstanding of policies or procedures

5. Of the following factors which contribute to possible undesirable public attitudes towards an agency, the one which is MOST susceptible to being changed by the efforts of the individual employee in an organization is that
    A. enforcement of unpopular regulations as offended many individuals
    B. the organization itself has an unsatisfactory reputation
    C. the public is not interested in agency matters
    D. there are many errors in judgment committed by individual subordinates

5.____

6. It is not enough for an agency's services to be of a high quality; attention must also be given to the acceptability of these services to the general public.
This statement is GENERALLY
    A. *false*; a superior quality of service automatically wins public support
    B. *true*; the agency cannot generally progress beyond the understanding and support of the public
    C. *false*; the acceptance by the public of agency services determines their quality
    D. *true*; the agency is generally unable to engage in any effective enforcement activity without public support

6.____

7. Sustained agency participation in a program sponsored by a community organization is MOST justified when
    A. the achievement of agency objectives in some area depends partly on the activity of this organization
    B. the community organization is attempting to widen the base of participation in all community affairs
    C. the agency is uncertain as to what the community wants
    D. the agency is uncertain as to what the community wants

7.____

8. Of the following, the LEAST likely way in which a records system may serve a supervisor is in
    A. developing a sympathetic and cooperative public attitude toward the agency
    B. improving the quality of supervision by permitting a check on the accomplishment of subordinates
    C. permit a precise prediction of the exact incidences in specific categories for the following year
    D. helping to take the guesswork out of the distribution of the agency

8.____

9. Assuming that the *grapevine* in any organization is virtually indestructible, the one of the following which it is MOST important for management to understand is:
   A. What is being spread by means of the *grapevine* and the reason for spreading it
   B. What is being spread by means of the *grapevine* and how it is being spread
   C. Who is involved in spreading the information that is on the *grapevine*
   D. Why those who are involved in spreading the information are doing so

10. When the supervisor writes a report concerning an investigation to which he has been assigned, it should be LEAST intended to provide
    A. a permanent official record of relevant information gathered
    B. a summary of case findings limited to facts which tend to indicate the guilt of a suspect
    C. a statement of the facts on which higher authorities may base a corrective or disciplinary action
    D. other investigators with information so that they may continue with other phases of the investigation

11. In survey work, questionnaires rather than interviews are sometimes used. The one of the following which is a DISADVANTAGE of the questionnaire method as compared with the interview is the
    A. difficulty of accurately interpreting the results
    B. problem of maintaining anonymity of the participant
    C. fact that it is relatively uneconomical
    D. requirement of special training for the distribution of questionnaires

12. In his contacts with the public, an employee should attempt to create a good climate of support for his agency.
    This statement is GENERALLY
    A. *false*; such attempts are clearly beyond the scope of his responsibility
    B. *true*; employees of an agency who come in contact with the public have the opportunity to affect public relations
    C. *false*; such activity should be restricted to supervisors trained in public relations techniques
    D. *true*; the future expansion of the agency depends to a great extent on continued public support of the agency

13. The repeated use by a supervisor of a call for volunteers to get a job done is objectionable MAINLY because it
    A. may create a feeling of animosity between the volunteers and the non-volunteers
    B. may indicate that the supervisor is avoiding responsibility for making assignments which will be most productive
    C. is an indication that the supervisor is not familiar with the individual capabilities of his men
    D. is unfair to men who, for valid reasons, do not, or cannot volunteer

14. Of the following statements concerning subordinates' expressions to a supervisor of their opinions and feelings concerning work situations, the one which is MOST correct is that
    A. by listening and responding to such expressions the supervisor encourages the development of complaints
    B. the lack of such expressions should indicate to the supervisor that there is a high level of job satisfaction
    C. the more the supervisor listens to and responds to such expressions, the more he demonstrates lack of supervisory ability
    D. by listening and responding to such expressions, the supervisor will enable many subordinates to understand and solve their own problems on the job

15. In attempting to motivate employees, rewards are considered preferable to punishment PRIMARILY because
    A. punishment seldom has any effect on human behavior
    B. punishment usually results in decreased production
    C. supervisors find it difficult to punish
    D. rewards are more likely to result in willing cooperation

16. In an attempt to combat the low morale in his organization, a high level supervisor publicized an *open-door policy* to allow employees who wished to do so to come to him with their complaints.
    Which of the following is LEAST likely to account for the fact that no employee came in with a complaint?
    A. Employees are generally reluctant to go over the heads of their immediate supervisor.
    B. The employees did not feel that management would help them.
    C. The low morale was not due to complaints associated with the job.
    D. The employees felt that they had more to lose than to gain.

17. It is MOST desirable to use written instructions rather than oral instructions for a particular job when
    A. a mistake on the job will not be serious
    B. the job can be completed in a short time
    C. there is no need to explain the job minutely
    D. the job involves many details

18. If you receive a telephone call regarding a matter which your office does not handle, you should FIRST
    A. give the caller the telephone number of the proper office so that he can dial again
    B. offer to transfer the caller to the proper office
    C. suggest that the caller re-dial since he probably dialed incorrectly
    D. tell the caller he has reached the wrong office and then hang up

19. When you answer the telephone, the MOST important reason for identifying yourself and your organization is to
    A. give the caller time to collect his or her thoughts
    B. impress the caller with your courtesy
    C. inform the caller that he or she has reached the right number
    D. set a business-like tone at the beginning of the conversation

20. As soon as you pick up the phone, a very angry caller begins immediately to complain about city agencies and *red tape*. He says that he has been shifted to two or three different offices. It turs out that he is seeking information which is not immediately available to you. You believe, you know, however, where it can be found.
    Which of the following actions is the BEST one for you to take?
    A. To eliminate all confusion, suggest that the caller write the agency stating explicitly what he wants.
    B. Apologize by telling the caller how busy city agencies now are, but also tell him directly that you do not have the information he needs.
    C. Ask for the caller's telephone number and assure him you will call back after you have checked further.
    D. Give the caller the name and telephone number of the person who might be able to help, but explain that you are not positive he will get results/

21. Which of the following approaches usually provides the BEST communication in the objectives and values of a new program which is to be introduced?
    A. A general written description of the program by the program manager for review by those who share responsibility
    B. An effective verbal presentation by the program manager to those affected
    C. Development of the plan and operational approach in carrying out thc program by the program manager assisted by his key subordinates
    D. Development of the plan by the program manager's supervisor

22. What is the BEST approach for introducing change?
    A
    A. combination of written and also verbal communication to all personnel affected by the change
    B. general bulletin to all personnel
    C. meeting pointing out all the values of the new approach
    D. written directive to key personnel

23. Of the following, committees are BEST used for
    A. advising the head of the organization
    B. improving functional work
    C. making executive decisions
    D. making specific planning decisions

24. An effective discussion leader is one who 24.____
    A. announces the problem and his preconceived solution at the start of the discussion
    B. guides and directs the discussion according to pre-arranged outline
    C. interrupts or corrects confused participants to save time
    D. permits anyone to say anything at any time

25. The human relations movement in management theory is basically concerned with 25.____
    A. counteracting employee unrest
    B. eliminating the *time and motion* man
    C. interrelationships among individuals in organizations
    D. the psychology of the worker

KEY (CORRECT ANSWERS)

1.	C		11.	A
2.	C		12.	B
3.	A		13.	B
4.	D		14.	D
5.	D		15.	D
6.	B		16.	C
7.	A		17.	D
8.	C		18.	B
9.	A		19.	C
10.	B		20.	C

21.	C
22.	A
23.	A
24.	B
25.	C

EXAMINATION SECTION

TEST 1

DIRECTIONS: Each question or incomplete statement is followed by several suggested answers or completions. Select the one that BEST answers the question or completes the statement. *PRINT THE LETTER OF THE CORRECT ANSWER IN THE SPACE AT THE RIGHT.*

1. Good procedure in handling complaints from the public may be divided into the following four principal stages:
   I. Investigation of the complaint
   II. Receipt of the complaint
   III. Assignment of responsibility for investigation and correction
   IV. Notification of correction

   The ORDER in which these stages ordinarily come is:
   A. III, II, I, IV   B. II, III, I, IV   C. II, III, IV, I   D. II, IV, III, I

   1._____

2. The department may expect the MOST severe public criticism if
   A. it asks for an increase in its annual budget
   B. it purchases new and costly street cleaning equipment
   C. sanitation officers and men are reclassified to higher salary grades
   D. there is delay in cleaning streets of snow

   2._____

3. The MOST important function of public relations in the department should be to
   A. develop cooperation on the part of the public in keeping streets clean
   B. get stricter penalties enacted for health code violations
   C. recruit candidates for entrance positions who ca be developed into supervisors
   D. train career personnel so that they can advance in the department

   3._____

4. The one of the following which has MOST frequently elicited unfavorable public comment has been
   A. dirty sidewalks or streets   B. dumping on lot
   C. failure to curb dogs   D. overflowing garbage cans

   4._____

5. It has been suggested that, as a public relations measure, sections hold *open house* for the public.
   The MOST effective time for this would be
   A. during the summer when children are not in school and can accompany their parents
   B. during the winter when show is likely to fall and the public can see snow removal preparations
   C. immediately after a heavy snow storm when department snow removal operations are in full progress
   D. when street sanitation is receiving general attention as during *Keep City Clean* week

   5._____

63

6. When a public agency conducts a public relations program, it is MOST likely to find that each recipient of its message will
   A. disagree with the basic purpose of the message if the officials are not well known to him
   B. accept the message if it is presented by someone perceived as having a definite intention to persuade
   C. ignore the message unless it is presented in a literate and clever manner
   D. give greater attention to certain portions of the message as a result of his individual and cultural differences

7. Following are three statements about public relations and communications:
   I. A person who seeks to influence public opinion can speed up a trend
   II. Mass communications is the exposure of a mass audience to an idea
   III. All media are equally effective in reaching opinion leaders
   Which of the following choices CORRECTLY classifies the above statements into those which are correct and those which are not?
   A. I and II are correct, but III is not.
   B. II and III are correct, but I is not.
   C. I and III are correct, but II is not.
   D. III is correct, but I and II are not.

8. Public relations experts say that MAXIMUM effect for a message results from
   A. concentrating in one medium
   B. ignoring mass media and concentrating on *opinion makers*
   C. presenting only those factors which support a given position
   D. using a combination of two or more of the available media

9. To assure credibility and avoid hostility, the public relations man MUST
   A. make certain his message is truthful, not evasive or exaggerated
   B. make sure his message contains some dire consequence if ignored
   C. repeat the message often enough so that it cannot be ignored
   D. try to reach as many people and groups as possible

10. The public relations man MUST be prepared to assume that members of his audience
    A. may have developed attitudes toward his proposals—favorable, neutral, or unfavorable
    B. will be immediately hostile
    C. will consider his proposals with an open mind
    D. will invariably need an introduction to his subject

11. The one of the following statements that is CORRECT is:
    A. When a stupid question is asked of you by the public, it should be disregarded
    B. If you insist on formality between you and the public, the public will not be able to ask stupid questions that cannot be answered
    C. The public should be treated courteously, regardless of how stupid their questions may be
    D. You should explain to the public how stupid their questions are

12. With regard to public relations, the MOST important item which should be emphasized in an employee training program is that
    A. each inspector is a public relations agent
    B. an inspector should give the public all the information it asks for
    C. it is better to make mistakes and give erroneous information than to tell the public that you do not know the correct answer to their problem
    D. public relations is so specialized a field that only persons specially trained in it should consider it

13. Members of the public frequently ask about departmental procedures. Of the following, it is BEST to
    A. advise the public to put the question in writing so that he can get a proper formal reply
    B. refuse to answer because this is a confidential matter
    C. explain the procedure as briefly as possible
    D. attempt to avoid the issue by discussing other matters

14. The effectiveness of a public relations program in a public agency such as the authority is BEST indicated by the
    A. amount of mass media publicity favorable to the policies of the authority
    B. morale of those employees who directly serve the patrons of the authority
    C. public's understanding and support of the authority's program and policies
    D. number of complaint received by the authority from patrons using its facilities

15. In an attempt to improve public opinion about a certain idea, the BEST course of action for an agency to take would be to present the
    A. clearest statements of the idea even though the language is somewhat technical
    B. idea as the result of long-term studies
    C. idea in association with something familiar to most people
    D. idea as the viewpoint of the majority leaders

16. The fundamental factor in any agency's community relations program is
    A. an outline of the objectives
    B. relations with the media
    C. the everyday actions of the employees
    D. a well-planned supervisory program

17. The FUNDAMENTAL factor in the success of a community relations program is
    A. true commitment by the community
    B. true commitment by the administration
    C. a well-planned, systematic approach
    D. the actions of individuals in their contacts with the public

18. The statement below which is LEAST correct is:
    A. Because of selection standards, the supervisor frequently encounters problems resulting from subordinates' inability to express themselves in the language of the profession.
    B. Distortion of the meaning of a communication is usually brought about by a failure to use language that has a precise meaning to others.
    C. The term *filtering* is the distortion or dilution of content of a communication that occurs as information is passed from individual to individual.
    D. The complexity of the *communications net* will directly affect.

19. Consider the following three statements that may or may not be CORRECT:
    I. In order to prevent the stifling of communications flow, supervisors should insist that employees use the formal communications network.
    II. Two-way communications are faster and more accurate than one-way communications.
    III. There is a direct correlation between the effectiveness of communications and the total setting in which they occur.
    The choice below which MOST accurately describes the above statement is:
    A. All three are correct.
    B. All three are incorrect.
    C. More than one statement is correct.
    D. Only one of the statements is correct.

20. The statement below which is MOST inaccurate is:
    A. The supervisor's most important tool in learning whether or not he is communicating well is feedback.
    B. Follow-up is essential if useful feedback is to be obtained.
    C. Subordinates are entitled, as a matter of right, to explanations from management concerning the reasons for orders or directives.
    D. A skilled supervisor is often able to use the grapevine to good advantage.

21. *Since concurrence by those affected is not sought, this kind of communication can be issued with relative ease.*
    The kind of communication being referred to in this quotation is
    A. autocratic   B. democratic   C. directive   D. free-rein

22. The statement below which is LEAST correct is:
    A. Clarity is more important in oral communicating than in written since the readers of a written communication can read it over again.
    B. Excessive use of abbreviations in written communications should be avoided.
    C. Short sentences with simple words are preferred over complex sentences and difficult words in a written communication.
    D. The *newspaper* style of writing ordinarily simplifies expression and facilitates understanding.

23. Which one of the following is the MOST important factor for the department to consider in building a good public image?
    A. A good working relationship with the news media
    B. An efficient community relations program
    C. An efficient system for handling citizen complaints
    D. The proper maintenance of facilities and equipment
    E. The behavior of individuals in their contacts with the public.

24. It has been said that the ability to communicate clearly and concisely is the MOST important single skill of the supervisor.
    Consider the following statements:
    I. The adage, *Actions speak louder than words*, has NO application in superior/subordinate communications since good communications are accomplished with words.
    II. The environment in which a communication takes place will *rarely* determine its effect.
    III. Words are symbolic representations which must be associated with past experience or else they are meaningless.
    The choice below which MOST accurately describes the above statements is:
    A. I, II, and III are correct.
    B. I and II are correct, but III is not.
    C. I and III are correct, but II is not.
    D. III is correct, but I and II are not.
    E. I, II, and III are incorrect.

25. According to expert opinion, the effectiveness of an organization is very dependent upon good upward, downward, and lateral communications. Lateral communications are most important to the activity of coordinating the efforts of organizational units. Before real communication can take place at any level, barriers to communication must be recognized, understood, and removed.
    Consider the following three statements:
    I. The *principal* barrier to good communications is a failure to establish empathy between sender and receiver.
    II. The difference in status or rank between the sender and receiver of a communication may be a communications barrier.
    III. Communications are easier if they travel upward from subordinate to superior
    The choice below which MOST accurately describes the above statements is:
    A. I, II and III are incorrect.   B. I and II are incorrect.
    C. I, II, and III are correct.   D. I and II are correct.
    E. I and III are incorrect.

KEY (CORRECT ANSWERS)

1. B
2. D
3. A
4. A
5. D

6. D
7. A
8. D
9. A
10. A

11. C
12. A
13. C
14. C
15. C

16. C
17. D
18. A
19. D
20. C

21. A
22. A
23. E
24. D
25. E

EXAMINATION SECTION
TEST 1

DIRECTIONS: Each question or incomplete statement is followed by several suggested answers or completions. Select the one that BEST answers the question or completes the statement. *PRINT THE LETTER OF THE CORRECT ANSWER IN THE SPACE AT THE RIGHT.*

1. The term *first-line supervisor* refers to the lowest level of supervision in an organization. A dilemma faced by the first-line supervisor is that he represents

    A. management
    B. labor
    C. management and labor
    D. neither management nor labor

    1.____

2. Management experts generally consider it advisable to give instructions orally, even though these instructions may later be put in writing for permanent reference.
The MAIN reason for this advice is that

    A. employees sometimes misplace written instructions
    B. explanations can be made in accordance with individual needs
    C. written instructions tend to be unclear and ambiguous
    D. employees resent being given instructions in writing

    2.____

3. Of the following, the BEST reason why a supervisor should NOT delegate a certain job to a subordinate is that

    A. he does not have any subordinate who can develop the skills needed to do the job
    B. it is easier and quicker to do it himself
    C. he knows it will be done correctly if he does it himself
    D. he enjoys doing it himself

    3.____

4. Of the following, the step which the supervisor should take FIRST in handling a complaint from a member of his staff is to

    A. gather background information relevant to the complaint
    B. establish tentative solutions or answers to the complaint
    C. determine the nature of the complaint as clearly and as fully as possible
    D. make a determination as to whether the complaint is valid

    4.____

5. Before a supervisor delegates one of the duties which he normally performs to a member of his staff, the FIRST thing he should do is

    A. determine the long-range purpose of the job
    B. determine exactly what tasks the job involves
    C. decide how long it takes him to do the job
    D. decide to whom he will assign the job

    5.____

6. When an employee is not sure of the intent of a policy statement, it is usually BEST for him to consult

    A. a fellow worker
    B. a member of the planning staff
    C. his supervisor
    D. the manual of procedures

    6.____

69

7. The MOST appropriate time for a supervisor to have a discussion with an employee who has violated an agency policy is

   A. as soon as possible after the violation has occurred
   B. after a cooling-off period has elapsed
   C. the day after the violation occurred
   D. during the next staff meeting

8. Of the following, the MOST appropriate use of staff conferences is to enable the supervisor to

   A. inform staff of the latest administrative policies
   B. obtain the benefits of collective thinking about a problem
   C. let staff know that he is aware of violations of personnel policies
   D. give dissatisfied employees a chance to voice their grievances

9. Of the following, a term used to describe how a supervisor may determine whether he is communicating effectively with his staff is called

   A. backlash   B. feedback
   C. implementation   D. delegation

10. False rumors about unpleasant possibilities such as employee cutbacks can do serious damage to morale. Most rumors of this kind in large organizations and public agencies are caused by

    A. over-permissiveness and general laxity of supervision
    B. a breakdown in communication between management and employees
    C. employees who distort the facts for their own purposes
    D. newspaper articles planted by special interest groups

11. Of the following, staff meetings are LEAST likely to be productive when

    A. only four or five people are present
    B. the chairman conducts the meeting in a formal manner
    C. discussion is kept to a minimum
    D. private discussions are not allowed

12. The one of the following persons who USUALLY would be classified as belonging to middle management is the

    A. senior clerk   B. agency head
    C. bureau director   D. deputy commissioner

13. Of the following, the BEST way for a person to develop competence as an interviewer is to

    A. attend lectures on interviewing techniques
    B. practice with employees on the job
    C. conduct interviews under the supervision of an experienced instructor
    D. attend a training course in counselling

14. Of the following, the type of employee who would PROBABLY expect to be given the most authority to use independent judgment is the

    A. chemical engineer
    B. clerical worker
    C. bookkeeper
    D. registered nurse

15. Assume that you are asked to study and report on employee turnover in several agency units which vary widely as to total number of employees and the number of employees involved in turnover.
    In order to present an accurate picture of turnover, your report should show, with regard to persons leaving, both actual numbers and

    A. central tendencies
    B. percentages
    C. raw data
    D. rounded totals

16. Many employees tend to resist a reorganization because they feel that their status and security are threatened. Of the following, the BEST way to make it easier for employees to accept the changes necessitated by reorganization is to

    A. introduce many changes at the same time
    B. give them a chance to participate in evaluating proposed changes
    C. keep the changes secret until they are put into effect
    D. have staff people who have had little contact with the affected employees initiate the changes

17. The MOST important reason for investigating every accident on the job is to

    A. find out who was responsible for the accident
    B. determine the organization's legal liability for the accident
    C. correct the conditions or actions which caused the accident
    D. discipline the employee who caused the accident

18. Research studies indicate that an important difference between high-production and low-production supervisors lies in their manner of handling mistakes.
    When subordinates make mistakes, the high-production supervisor PROBABLY would

    A. concentrate on fixing responsibility and determining the subordinate's excuse for the mistake
    B. take over the assignment himself in order to avoid recurrence of the mistake
    C. look upon the mistake as an opportunity to provide training
    D. give the assignment to a subordinate who is not likely to repeat the mistake

19. The use of statistical controls is generally considered to be one of management's most effective means of determining what is happening at the operating level of an agency.
    Of the following, statistical controls are LEAST useful for

    A. furthering coordination
    B. measuring morale
    C. setting standards
    D. pinpointing responsibility

20. A basic problem of the supervisor is how to motivate employees. One approach is to 20._____
internalize motivation by providing opportunities for employees to derive satisfaction from
the work itself.
Of the following, internalized motivation would be the LEAST effective approach where
the employee

   A. enjoys autonomy because of the nature of the job
   B. accepts the organization's objectives
   C. makes the job his central life focus
   D. does a routine or assembly line job

KEY (CORRECT ANSWERS)

1. C	11. C
2. B	12. C
3. A	13. C
4. C	14. A
5. B	15. B
6. C	16. B
7. A	17. C
8. B	18. C
9. B	19. B
10. B	20. D

TEST 2

DIRECTIONS: Each question or incomplete statement is followed by several suggested answers or completions. Select the one that BEST answers the question or completes the statement. *PRINT THE LETTER OF THE CORRECT ANSWER IN THE SPACE AT THE RIGHT.*

1. Of the following, the BEST time for a supervisor to give advice about a job-related problem which a subordinate has brought up during an interview is USUALLY after the

    A. subordinate has told him all the facts
    B. supervisor has determined the employee's unconscious motives for bringing up the problem
    C. employee has submitted a written report on the problem
    D. supervisor has discussed the problem with his superior

    1._____

2. Of the following, the situation in which a supervisor would have to make the GREATEST effort in order to communicate effectively with his subordinates would occur when

    A. there is a large gap between the supervisor's background and experience and that of his subordinates
    B. the subordinates have already learned about the information through informal channels
    C. the subordinates have completed their education much more recently than the supervisor
    D. the supervisor has been with the organization for a much shorter time than most of his subordinates

    2._____

3. Of the following, the factor which would be MOST critical in influencing whether subordinates accept or resent a supervisor's authority is the

    A. manner in which the supervisor uses his authority
    B. frequency with which the supervisor ignores minor violations of rules
    C. degree of delegation to subordinates by the supervisor
    D. cultural attitudes of individual subordinates toward authority

    3._____

4. In which one of the following situations would employees be MOST likely to accept temporarily difficult working conditions without excessive complaining?

    A. The organization has a strict policy of disciplinary action against uncooperative employees.
    B. Employees do not have the right to take part in *job actions* or strikes.
    C. An atmosphere of mutual trust and good human relations exists between subordinates and managerial personnel.
    D. Relationships between subordinates and managerial personnel are strictly businesslike.

    4._____

5. Assume that an agency has been reorganized into integrated work teams. Instead of assigning employees performing the same task to a single unit, such as a typing pool, those performing different but interdependent parts of an activity are put into the same work group.
    Of the following, the MOST probable result of such a reorganization would be to

    A. permit more efficient work scheduling
    B. achieve greater economy
    C. decrease training costs
    D. improve employee job satisfaction

    5._____

6. The need for identification with a work group has been found to be one of the most powerful on-the-job motivations.
Of the following, the employee who is LEAST likely to have a strong attachment to his work group is one who

   A. is at the very bottom of the organization's promotional ladder
   B. belongs to a small department
   C. works with others of similar background and interests
   D. has worked for the organization for a considerable period of time

7. According to many management experts, the one of the following situations which would be the MOST significant indication that employees of an organization are dissatisfied with their supervisors and feel that they are being treated unfairly is one in which

   A. employees submit a large number of work-related suggestions
   B. many employees are unproductive and seem to be continually loafing on the job
   C. union membership has recently increased
   D. turnover is low in spite of a comparatively good labor market

8. A supervisor who has informal, friendly relationships with his subordinates is conducting himself

   A. *appropriately;* good informal relationships set the stage for better communication between the supervisor and subordinates on work-related problems
   B. *inappropriately;* subordinates who have informal relationships with their supervisor are not likely to accept his authority
   C. *appropriately;* friendly relationships between the supervisor and his subordinates will create a true feeling of equality between them
   D. *inappropriately;* subordinates are likely to become suspicious of insincerity and fearful of being manipulated

9. Specialization is a commonly-used method of increasing productivity and efficiency in a large organization. Task specialization means that separate and comparatively simple parts of a more complex job are performed by different employees.
Of the following, this type of specialization probably would NOT

   A. reduce training costs
   B. permit the use of more specialized equipment
   C. simplify the development of job controls
   D. give most employees a greater sense of accomplishment

10. Some management experts who have studied informal communication patterns in large organizations believe that the office grapevine is an effective means of communication.
Of the following, an IMPORTANT function performed by the grapevine is to

    A. permit feedback and spread information faster than most formal communication systems
    B. give employees important information from reliable sources
    C. permit management to identify rumor-mongers and troublemakers
    D. bring informal leaders to the attention of management

11. Recent studies of morale and productivity tend to show that

    A. the correlation between morale and productivity is rather low
    B. high morale is associated with high productivity
    C. low morale is associated with high productivity
    D. low morale is associated with low productivity

12. Research studies have indicated that teamwork among employees is MOST likely to result in higher productivity in a situation where

    A. employees accept as legitimate management's demands for higher productivity
    B. management strongly encourages the workers' demands spirit
    C. employees are unified for the purpose of protecting themselves against management's demands
    D. management does not encourage employees to make independent decisions

13. The relationship between boredom on the job and fatigue is CORRECTLY stated as follows:

    A. Boredom usually results in increased fatigue
    B. A worker usually becomes bored when he expends a minimum of physical energy
    C. Fatigue usually results in boredom
    D. A worker who is bored does not usually become fatigued

14. The *halo effect* can PROPERLY be suspected of harming supervisor-subordinate relationships when the supervisor

    A. does not discriminate between the good and poor work of an employee considered by him to be generally superior
    B. expects his subordinates to treat him in an impersonal and formal manner
    C. hesitates to discipline employees because of an extreme need for them to like him
    D. is unable to gain his employees' confidence because he cannot shed his reputation for being hardboiled and unfair

15. It is generally considered that the best interview is the one in which the interviewer talks less than the person interviewed.
    The one of the following which is an EFFECTIVE device to encourage the other person to talk during the interview is for the interviewer to

    A. summarize the feelings the person has expressed, omitting details and incidentals
    B. keep silent and show no indication of his reaction to what the person is saying
    C. clearly show his approval or disapproval of what the person is saying
    D. talk to the person in terms of concepts rather than specifics

16. Studies of groups of workers doing the same job under the same conditions have shown that there are always a few workers who have more accidents than the rest. The one of the following which is LEAST likely to be a finding of such studies is that those who have the MOST accidents PROBABLY are

    A. middle-aged
    B. poorly adjusted to work
    C. inexperienced at the job
    D. less efficient than other workers

17. Work measurement has been defined as *the determination of the proper amount of time and effort required for the effective performance of a specific task.*
Of the following, the factor which would be LEAST relevant in studying an operation by means of work measurement is whether the operation is

    A. repetitive with constant standards of quality
    B. compensated for at a prevailing rate of pay
    C. routine in nature and relatively easy to perform
    D. performed in large volume

18. Of the following, *participative management* can be defined BEST as a method in which

    A. subordinates have formed groups for the purpose of gaining participation in the decisions of management
    B. management makes a practice of encouraging subordinates as a group to discuss and participate in decisions on a wide variety of work-related problems
    C. managerial employees are given varied assignments on a rotating basis
    D. management gives all employees the opportunity to participate in major policy decisions

19. *Internalized motivation* has been described as a method of motivating employees by enabling them to derive satisfaction through doing the job itself. This approach to motivating employees would require management to

    A. assume that most employees like work and enjoy doing a good job
    B. encourage competition among employees for promotions and higher salaries
    C. emphasize improved fringe benefits and conditions of work
    D. consider employee needs to be more important than organizational needs

20. If a supervisor should find that he must issue an order his subordinates will probably resist, it is advisable for the supervisor to FIRST

    A. discuss the order with his subordinates and give them an opportunity to ask questions and make objections
    B. issue the order without comment and discourage discussion and objections by his subordinates
    C. inform his subordinates that he does not agree with the order he is going to give them, but must carry out the decisions of higher authority
    D. inform his subordinates that he will take disciplinary action against those who resist carrying out the order he will present to them

21. When a supervisor finds that his subordinates differ considerably in the amount of attention and guidance they require of him, it would be MOST advisable for the supervisor to

    A. adjust his supervisory practices according to individual needs
    B. give an equal amount of attention and guidance to each subordinate in order to be fair
    C. give less responsibility to subordinates who seek assistance
    D. permit employees who prefer independence to work strictly on their own

22. Connecting lines on an organization chart represent lines of 22._____

    A. management quality controls
    B. work flow
    C. authority and responsibility
    D. fiscal accountability

23. *General supervision* has been defined as a method in which the supervisor makes 23._____
    assignments in broad, general terms and gives considerable autonomy to subordinates,
    in accordance with their knowledge and abilities.
    A supervisor who uses this method is LEAST likely to

    A. do different work from that of subordinates
    B. concentrate on long-range problems
    C. exert excessive pressure on subordinates
    D. devote considerable effort to training subordinates

24. Of the following, the MOST important reason why a supervisor should be cautious about 24._____
    giving subordinates advice about personal problems is that the

    A. subordinate may blame him if the advice turns out to be misleading
    B. supervisor should not discuss personal problems with subordinates on office time
    C. subordinate may lose confidence in his ability to perform on the job
    D. supervisor may not know enough to give helpful advice

25. Professional or technical consultants may be used MOST appropriately by a human ser- 25._____
    vices agency to

    A. direct staff conferences centered around programs
    B. give advice regarding the quality of service or the effectiveness of plans
    C. supervise implementation of programs they have developed
    D. direct the in-service training program

KEY (CORRECT ANSWERS)

1. A
2. A
3. A
4. C
5. D

6. A
7. B
8. A
9. D
10. A

11. A
12. A
13. A
14. A
15. A

16. A
17. B
18. B
19. A
20. A

21. A
22. C
23. C
24. D
25. B

EXAMINATION SECTION
TEST 1

DIRECTIONS: Each question or incomplete statement is followed by several suggested answers or completions. Select the one that BEST answers the question or completes the statement. *PRINT THE LETTER OF THE CORRECT ANSWER IN THE SPACE AT THE RIGHT.*

1. It is generally accepted that, of the following, the MOST important medium for developing integration and continuity in learning on the job is
   A. day-to-day experience on the job
   B. the supervisory conference
   C. the staff meeting
   D. the professional seminar

   1.____

2. Assume that you find that one of your workers is over-identifying with a particular client.
   Of the following, the MOST appropriate step for you to take FIRST in dealing with this situation is to
   A. transfer the cases to another worker
   B. inform the worker that he cannot give satisfactory service if he over-identifies with a client
   C. interview the client yourself to determine his feelings about his relationship with the worker
   D. arrange a conference with the worker to discuss the reasons for her over-identification with this client

   2.____

3. The one of the following which is the MOST likely reason why a newly-appointed supervisor would have a tendency to interfere actively in a relationship between one of his workers and a client is that the supervisor
   A. has unresolved feelings about relinquishing the role of worker, and has not yet accepted his role as supervisor
   B. must give direct assistance in the situation because the worker cannot handle it
   C. is attempting to share with his worker the knowledge and skill which he has developed in direct practice
   D. has not realized that immediate responsibility for work with clients has been delegated to others

   3.____

4. A worker who has a tendency to resist authority and supervision can be helped MOST effectively if, of the following, the supervisor
   A. behaves in a strict and impersonal manner so that the worker will accept his authority as a supervisor
   B. modifies the relationship so that he will be less authoritarian and threatening to the worker
   C. gives the worker a simple, matter-of-fact interpretation of the supervisory relationship and has an understanding acceptance of the worker's response
   D. temporarily establishes a peer relationship with the worker in order to overcome his resistance

   4.____

5. Before interviewing a newly-appointed worker for the first time, of the following, it is DESIRABLE for the supervisor to
    A. learn as much as he can about the worker's background and interests in order to eliminate the routine of asking questions and eliciting answers
    B. review the job information to be covered in order to make it easier to be impersonal and keep to the business at hand
    C. send the worker orientation material about the agency and the job and ask him to study it before the interview
    D. review available information about the worker in order to find an area of shared experience to serve as a *taking off* point for getting acquainted

5._____

6. In interviewing a new worker, of the following, it is IMPORTANT for the supervisor to
    A. give direction to the progress of the interview and maintain a leadership role throughout
    B. allow the worker to take the initiative in order to give him full scope for freedom of expression
    C. maintain a non-directional approach so that the worker will reveal his true attitudes and feelings
    D. avoid interrupting the worker, even though he seems to want to do all the talking

6._____

7. When a new worker, during his first few days, shows such symptoms of insecurity as *stage fright*, helpless immobility, or extreme talkativeness, of the following, it would be MOST helpful for the supervisor to
    A. start the worker out on some activity in which he is relatively secure
    B. ignore the symptoms and allow the worker to *sink or swim* on his own
    C. have a conference with the worker and interpret to him the reasons for his feelings of insecurity
    D. consider the probability that this worker may not be suited for a profession which requires skill in interpersonal relationships

7._____

8. Of the following, the MOST desirable method of minimizing workers' dependence on the supervisor and encouraging self-dependence is to
    A. hold group instead of individual supervisory conferences at regular intervals
    B. schedule individual supervisory conferences only in response to the workers' obvious need for guidance
    C. plan for progressive exposure to other opportunities for learning afforded by the agency and the community
    D. allow workers to learn by trial and error rather than by direct supervisory guidance

8._____

9. Of the following, it would NOT be appropriate for the supervisor to use early supervisory conferences with the new workers as a means of
    A. giving him direct practical help in order to get going on the job
    B. estimating the level of his native abilities, professional skills and experience
    C. getting clues as to his characteristic ways of learning in a new situation
    D. assessing his potential for future supervisory responsibility

9._____

10. Without careful planning by the supervisor for orientation of the new worker, an informal system of orientation by co-workers inevitably develops.
    Such an informal system of orientation is USUALLY
    A. *beneficial*, because many new workers learn more readily when instructed by their peers
    B. *harmful*, because informal orientation by an undesignated co-worker can lead a new worker astray instead of helping him
    C. *beneficial*, because assumption by subordinates of responsibility for orientation will free the supervisor for other urgent work
    D. *harmful*, because such informal orientation by a co-worker will tend to destroy the authority of the supervisor

11. Of the following, the BEST way for a supervisor to assist a subordinate who has unusual work pressures is to
    A. relieve him of some of his cases until the pressures subside
    B. help him to decide which cases should be given the most attention during the period of pressure, and how to provide coverage for less urgent cases
    C. inform him that he must learn to tolerate and adjust to such pressures
    D. point out that he should learn to understand the causes of the pressures, which probably resulted from his own deficiencies

12. Many supervisors have a tendency to use case records mainly for the purpose of analysis of the workers' skill or evaluation of their performance.
    Of the following, a PROBABLE result of this practice is that
    A. workers are likely to tie-in recording with supervisory evaluation of their work, without giving proper emphasis to their importance in improving service to clients
    B. the worker is likely to devote an inordinate amount of time to case records at the expense of his clients
    C. the records are likely to be too lengthy and detailed, limiting their value for other important purposes
    D. the records are likely to be of little value for administrative and research purposes

13. A common obstacle to adequate recording in a large social work agency is the fact that many workers consider recording to be a time-consuming chore. In order to obtain the cooperation of staff in keeping proper records, of the following, it is MOST important for an agency to provide
    A. indisputable evidence of the intelligent use of records as tools in formulating policy and improving service
    B. a system of checks and controls to assure that workers are preparing adequate and timely records
    C. adequate clerical services and mechanical equipment for recording
    D. sufficient time for recording in the organization of every job

14. The one of the following which is NOT a purpose of keeping case records in an agency is
    A. planning   B. research
    C. training   D. job classification

4 (#1)

15. When a supervisor is reviewing the records of a worker, of the following, he should plan to read
    A. records of new cases only, following up each interview selectively
    B. the total caseload, in order to determine which aspects of the worker's performance should be examined
    C. those records which the worker has brought to the supervisor's attention because of the need for help
    D. a block of records selected according to the worker's need for help, and some records selected at random

15.____

16. The one of the following which is the PRIMARY purpose of the regular staff meeting in an agency is
    A. initiation of action in order to get the agency's work done
    B. staff training and development
    C. program and policy determination
    D. communication of new policies and procedures

16.____

17. Of the following, group supervision in an agency is intended as a means of
    A. strengthening the total supervisory process
    B. shifting the focus of supervision from the individual to the group
    C. saving costs in terms of time and manpower
    D. influencing policy through group interaction

17.____

18. The supervisor's job brings him closer to such limiting factors in the operation of an agency as faulty administrative structure, shortage of funds and lack of facilities, inadequacies in personnel practices, community pressures, and excessive workload.
    For the supervisor to make a practice of communicating to his subordinates his feelings of frustration about such limitations in the work setting would be
    A. *appropriate*, because the worker will be more understanding of the supervisor's burdens and frustrations
    B. *inappropriate*, because the climate created will block rather than further the purposes of supervision
    C. *appropriate*, because such communication will create a more democratic climate between the worker and the supervisor
    D. *inappropriate*, because the supervisor must support and condone agency policies and practices in the presence of subordinates

18.____

19. A suggestion has been made that the teaching and administrative functions of supervision should be separated, so that the supervisor responsible for teaching would not be responsible for evaluation of the same workers.
    The one of the following which is the MOST important reason for this point of view is that
    A. elements that confer on the supervisor a position of authority and power unduly threaten the learning situation
    B. teaching skill and administrative ability do not usually go together

19.____

C. a supervisor who has been responsible for training a worker is likely to be prejudiced in his favor
D. performance evaluation and total job accountability should be two separate functions

20. In reviewing a worker's cases in preparation for a periodic evaluation, you note that she has done a uniformly good job with certain types of cases and poor work with other types of cases.
Of the following, the BEST approach for you to take in this situation is to
    A. bring this to the worker's attention, find out why she favors certain types of clients, and discuss ways in which she can improve her service to all clients
    B. bring this to the worker's attention and suggest that she may need professional counseling, as she seems to be blocked in working with certain types of cases
    C. assign to her mainly those cases which she handles best and transfer the types of cases which she handles poorly to another worker
    D. accept the fact that a worker cannot be expected to give uniformly good service to all clients, and take no further action

20.____

KEY (CORRECT ANSWERS)

1.	B	11.	B
2.	D	12.	A
3.	A	13.	A
4.	C	14.	D
5.	D	15.	D
6.	A	16.	A
7.	A	17.	A
8.	C	18.	B
9.	D	19.	A
10.	B	20.	A

TEST 2

DIRECTIONS: Each question or incomplete statement is followed by several suggested answers or completions. Select the one that BEST answers the question or completes the statement. *PRINT THE LETTER OF THE CORRECT ANSWER IN THE SPACE AT THE RIGHT.*

1. Of the following, the choice of method to be used in the supervisory process should be influenced MOST by the
   A. number and type of cases carried by each worker
   B. emotional maturity of the worker
   C. number of workers supervised and their past experience
   D. subject matter to be learned and the long-range goals of supervision

   1._____

2. In an evaluation conference with a worker, the BEST approach for the supervisor to take is to
   A. help the worker to identify his strengths as a basis for working on his weaknesses
   B. identify the worker's weaknesses and help him overcome them
   C. allow the worker to identify his weaknesses first and then suggest ways of overcoming them
   D. discuss the worker's weaknesses but emphasize his strengths

   2._____

3. Assume that a worker is discouraged about the progress of his work and feels that it is futile to attempt to cope with many of his cases.
   Of the following, it would be BEST for the supervisor to
   A. suggest to the worker that such feelings are inappropriate for a professional worker
   B. tell the worker that he must seek professional help in order to overcome these feelings
   C. reduce the worker's caseload and give him cases that are less complex
   D. review with the worker several of his cases in which there were obvious accomplishments

   3._____

4. The supervisor is responsible for providing the worker with the following means of support, with the EXCEPTION of
   A. interest and advice on his personal problems
   B. instruction on community resources
   C. inspiration for carrying out the work of the agency
   D. understanding his strengths and limitations

   4._____

5. When a worker frequently takes the initiative in asking questions and discussing problems during a supervisory conference, this is PROBABLY an indication that the
   A. supervisor is not sufficiently interested in the work
   B. conference is a positive learning experience for the worker
   C. worker is hostile and resists supervision
   D. supervisor's position of authority is in question

   5._____

84

2 (#2)

6. When a supervisor finds that one of his workers cannot accept criticism, of the following, it would be BEST for the supervisor to
   A. have the worker transferred to another supervisor
   B. warn the worker of disciplinary proceedings unless his attitude changes
   C. have the worker suspended after explaining the reason
   D. explore with the worker his attitude toward authority

7. Of the following, the condition which the inexperienced worker is LEAST likely to be aware of, without the guidance of the supervisor, is
   A. when he is successful in helping a client
   B. when he is not making progress in helping a client
   C. that he has a personal bias toward certain clients
   D. that he feels insecure because of lack of experience

8. The supervisor should provide an inexperienced worker with controls as well as freedom MAINLY because controls will
   A. enable him to set up his own controls sooner
   B. put him in a situation which is closer to the realities of life
   C. help him to use authority in handling a casework problem
   D. give him a feeling of security and lay the foundation for future self-direction

9. A result of the use of summarized case recording by the worker is that it
   A. gives the supervisor more responsibility for selecting cases to discuss in conference
   B. makes more time available for other activities
   C. lowers the morale of many workers
   D. decreases discussion of cases by the worker and the supervisor

10. The distinction between the role of professional workers and the role of auxiliary or sub-professional workers in an agency is based upon the
    A. position within the agency hierarchy
    B. amount of close supervision given
    C. emergent nature of tasks assigned
    D. functions performed

11. Of the following, the MOST important source of learning for the worker should be
    A. departmental directives and professional literature
    B. his co-workers in the agency
    C. the content of in-service training courses
    D. the clients in his caseload

12. A client is MOST likely to feel that he is receiving acceptance and understanding if the social worker
    A. gets detailed information about the client's problem
    B. demonstrates that he realistically understands the client's problem
    C. has an intellectual understanding of the client's problem
    D. offers the client assurance of assistance

13. A client will be MORE encouraged to speak freely about his problems if the worker
    A. avoids asking too many questions
    B. asks leading rather than pointed questions
    C. suggests possible answers
    D. identifies with the client

14. A client would be MOST likely to be able to accept help in a time of crisis and need if the worker
    A. explains agency policy to him
    B. responds immediately to the client's need
    C. explains why help cannot be given immediately
    D. reaches out to help the client establish his rightful claim for assistance

15. It is a generally accepted principle that the worker should interpret for himself what the client is saying, but usually should not pass his interpretation on to the client because the client
    A. will become hostile to the worker
    B. should arrive at his own conclusions at his own pace
    C. must request the interpretation first
    D. usually wants facts, rather than the worker's interpretation

16. In evaluating the client's capacity to cope with his problems, it is MOST important for the worker to assess his ability to
    A. form close relationships
    B. ask for help
    C. express his hostility
    D. verbalize his difficulties

17. When a worker finds that he disagrees strongly with an agency policy, it is DESIRABLE for him to
    A. share his feelings about the policy with his client
    B. understand fully why he has such strong feelings about the policy
    C. refer cases involving the policy to his supervisor
    D. refuse to give help in cases involving the policy

18. Which of the following practices is BEST for a supervisor to use when assigning work to his staff?
    A. Give workers with seniority the most difficult jobs
    B. Assign all unimportant work to the slower workers
    C. Permit each employee to pick the job he prefers
    D. Make assignments based on the workers' abilities

19. In which of the following instances is a supervisor MOST justified in giving commands to people under his supervision?
    When
    A. they delay in following instructions which have been given to them clearly
    B. they become relaxed and slow about work, and he wants to speed up their production
    C. he must direct them in an emergency situation
    D. he is instructing them on jobs that are unfamiliar to them

20. Which of the following supervisory actions or attitudes is MOST likely to result in getting subordinates to try to do as much work as possible for a supervisor?
    He
    A. shows that his most important interest is in schedules and production goals
    B. consistently pressures his staff to get the work out
    C. never fails to let them know he is in charge
    D. considers their abilities and needs while requiring that production goals be met

KEY (CORRECT ANSWERS)

1.	D	11.	D
2.	A	12.	B
3.	D	13.	D
4.	A	14.	D
5.	B	15.	B
6.	D	16.	A
7.	C	17.	B
8.	D	18.	D
9.	B	19.	C
10.	D	20.	D

TEST 3

DIRECTIONS: Each question or incomplete statement is followed by several suggested answers or completions. Select the one that BEST answers the question or completes the statement. *PRINT THE LETTER OF THE CORRECT ANSWER IN THE SPACE AT THE RIGHT.*

1. One of your workers comes to you and complains in an angry manner about your having chosen him for some particular assignment. In your opinion, the subject of the complaint is trivial land unimportant, but it seems to be quite important to your worker.
   The BEST of the following actions for you to take in this situation is to
   A. allow the worker to continue talking until he has calmed down and then explain the reasons for your having chosen him for that particular assignment
   B. warn the worker to moderate his tone of voice at once because he is bordering on insubordination
   C. tell the worker in a friendly tone that he is making a tremendous fuss over an extremely minor matter
   D. point out to the worker that you are his immediate supervisor and that you are running the unit in accordance with official policy

2. The one of the following which is the LEAST desirable action for an assistant supervisor to take in disciplining a subordinate for an infraction of the rules is to
   A. caution him against repetition of the infraction, even if it is minor
   B. point out his progress in applying the rules at the same time that you reprimand him
   C. be as specific as possible in reprimanding him for rule infractions
   D. allow a cooling-off period to elapse before reprimanding him

3. A training program for workers assigned to the intake section should include actual practice in simulated interviews under simulated conditions.
   The one of the following educational principles which is the CHIEF justification for this statement is that
   A. the workers will remember what they see better and longer than what they read or hear
   B. the workers will learn more effectively by actually doing the act themselves than they would learn from watching others do it
   C. the conduct of simulated interviews once or twice will enable them to cope with the real situation with little difficulty
   D. a training program must employ methods of a practical nature if the workers are to find anything of lasting value in it

4. In order for a supervisor to employ the system of democratic leadership in his supervision, it would generally be BEST for him to
   A. allow his subordinates to assist in deciding on methods of work performance and job assignments but only in those areas where decisions have not been made on higher administrative levels

B. allow his subordinates to decide how to do the required work, interposing his authority when work is not completed on schedule or is improperly completed
C. attempt to make assignments of work to individuals only of the type which they enjoy doing
D. maintain control over job assignment and work production, but allow the subordinates to select methods of work and internal conditions of work at democratically conducted staff conferences

5. In a unit in which supervision has been considered quite effective, it has become necessary to press for above-normal production for a limited period to achieve a required goal.
   The one of the following which is a LEAST likely result of this pressure is that
   A. there will be more *griping* by employees
   B. some workers will do both more and better work than has been normal for them
   C. there will be an enhanced feeling of group unity
   D. there will be increased absenteeism

6. For a supervisor to encourage competitive feelings among his staff is
   A. *advisable*, chiefly because the workers will perform more efficiently when they have proper motivation
   B. *inadvisable*, chiefly because the workers will not perform well under the pressure of competition
   C. *advisable*, chiefly because the workers will have a greater incentive to perform their job properly
   D. *inadvisable*, chiefly because the workers may focus their attention on areas where they excel and neglect other essential aspects of the job

7. In selecting jobs to be assigned to a new worker, the supervisor should assign those jobs which
   A. give the worker the greatest variety of experience
   B. offer the worker the greatest opportunity to achieve concrete results
   C. present the worker with the greatest stimulation because of their interesting nature
   D. require the least amount of contact with outside agencies

8. A supervisor should avoid a detailed discussion of a worker-client interview with a new worker before the worker has fully recorded the interview CHIEFLY because such a discussion might
   A. cover matters which are already fully covered and explained in the written record
   B. make the worker forget some important deal learned during the interview
   C. color the recording according to the worker's reaction to his supervisor's opinions
   D. minimize the worker's feeling of having reached a decision independently

9. Some supervisors encourage their worker to submit a list of their questions about specific jobs or their comments about problems they wish to discuss in advance of the worker-supervisor conference.
   This practice is
   A. *desirable*, chiefly because it helps to stimulate and focus the worker's thinking about his caseload
   B. *undesirable*, chiefly because it will stifle the worker's free expression of his problems and attitudes
   C. *desirable*, chiefly because it will allow the conference to move along more smoothly and quickly
   D. *undesirable*, chiefly because it will restrict the scope of the conference and the variety of jobs discussed

10. An alert supervisor hears a worker apparently giving the wrong information to a client and immediately reprimands him severely.
    For the supervisor to reprimand the worker at his point is poor CHIEFLY because
    A. instruction must precede correct performance
    B. oral reprimands are less effective than written reprimands
    C. the worker was given no opportunity to explain his reasons for what he did
    D. more effective training can be obtained by discussing the errors with a group of workers

11. The one of the following circumstances when it would generally be MOST proper for a supervisor to do a job himself rather than to train a subordinate to do the job is when it is
    A. a job which the supervisor enjoys doing and does well
    B. not a very time-consuming job but an important one
    C. difficult to train another to do the job, yet is not difficult for the supervisor to do
    D. unlikely that this or any similar job will have to be done again at any future time

12. Effective training of subordinates requires that the supervisor understand certain facts about learning and forgetting processes.
    Among these is the fact that people GENERALLY
    A. forget what they learned at a much greater rate during the first day than during subsequent periods
    B. both learn and forget at a relatively constant rate and this rate is dependent upon their general intellectual capacity
    C. learn at a relatively constant rate except for periods of assimilation when the quantity of retained learning decreases while information is becoming firmly fixed in the mind
    D. learn very slowly at first when introduced to a new topic, after which there is a great increase in the rate of learning

13. It has been suggested that a subordinate who likes his superior will tend to do better work than one who does not.
    According to the MOST widely held current theories of supervision, this suggestion is a
    A. *bad* one, since personal relationships tend to interfere with proper professional relationships
    B. *bad* one, since the strongest motivating factors are fear and uncertainty
    C. *good* one, since liking one's superior is a motivating factor for good work performance
    D. *good* one, since liking one's supervisor is the most important factor in employee performance

14. One factor which might be given consideration in deciding upon the optimum span of control of a supervisor over his immediate subordinates is the position of the supervisor in the hierarchy of the organization.
    It is generally considered proper that the number of subordinates immediately supervised by a higher, upper echelon supervisor _____ the number supervised by lower level supervisors.
    A. is unrelated to and tends to form no pattern with
    B. should be about the same as
    C. should be larger than
    D. should be smaller than

15. The one of the following instances when it is MOST important for an upper level supervisor to follow the chain of command is when he is
    A. communicating decisions
    B. communicating information
    C. receiving suggestions
    D. seeking information

16. At the end of his probationary period, a supervisor should be considered potentially valuable in his position if he shows
    A. awareness of his areas of strength and weakness, identification with the administration of the department, and ability to learn under supervision
    B. skill in work, supervision, and administration, and a friendly democratic approach to the staff
    C. knowledge of departmental policies and procedures and ability to carry them out, ability to use authority, and ability to direct the work of the staff
    D. an identification with the department, acceptance of responsibility, and ability to give help to the individuals who are to be supervised

17. Good supervision is selective because
    A. it is not necessary to direct all the activities of the person
    B. a supervisor would never have time to know the whole caseload of a worker
    C. workers resent too much help from a supervisor
    D. too much reading is a waste of valuable time

18. An important administrative problem is how precisely to define the limits of authority that is delegated to subordinate supervisors.
Such definition of limits of authority should be
   A. as precise as possible and practicable in all areas
   B. as precise as possible and practicable in areas of function, but should allow considerable flexibility in the area of personnel management
   C. as precise as possible and practicable in the area
   D. of personnel management, but should allow considerable flexibility in the areas of function
   E. in general terms so as to allow considerable flexibility both in the areas of function and in the areas of personnel management

19. Experts in the field of personnel relations feel that it is generally a bad practice for subordinate employees to become aware of pending or contemplated changes in policy or organizational set-up via the *grapevine* CHIEFLY because
   A. evidence that one or more responsible officials have proved untrustworthy will undermine confidence in the agency
   B. the information disseminated by this method is seldom entirely accurate and generally spreads needless unrest among the subordinate staff
   C. the subordinate staff may conclude that the administration feels the staff cannot be trusted with the true information
   D. the subordinate staff may conclude that the administration lacks the courage to make an unpopular announcement through official channels

20. Supervision is subject to many interpretations, depending on the area in which it functions.
Of the following, the statement which represents the MOST appropriate meaning of supervision as it is known in social work practice is that it
   A. is a leadership process for the development of new leaders
   B. is an educational and administrative process aimed at teaching personnel the goal of improved service to the client
   C. is an activity aimed chiefly at insuring that workers will adhere to all agency directives
   D. provides the opportunity for administration to secure staff reaction to agency policies

21. A supervisor may utilize various methods in the supervisory process.
The one of the following upon which sound supervisory practice rests in the selection of supervisory techniques is
   A. an estimate of the worker arrived at through current and past evaluation of performance as well as through worker's participation
   B. the previous supervisor's evaluation and recommendation
   C. the worker's expression of his personal preference for certain types of experience
   D. the amount of time available to supervisor and supervisee

22. It is the practice of some supervisors, when they believe that it would be desirable for a subordinate to take a particular action in a case, to inform the subordinate of this in the form of a suggestion rather than in the form of a direct order.
In general, this method of getting a subordinate to take the desired action is
   A. *inadvisable*; it may create in the mind of the subordinate the impression that the supervisor is uncertain about the efficacy of her plan and is trying to avoid whatever responsibility she may have in resolving the case
   B. *advisable*; it provides the subordinate with the maximum opportunity to use her own judgment in handling the case
   C. *inadvisable*; it provides the subordinate with no clear-cut direction and, therefore, is likely to leave her with a feeling of uncertainty and frustration
   D. *advisable*; it presents the supervisor's view in a manner which will be most likely to evoke the subordinate's cooperation

22.____

23. A veteran supervisor noticed that one of her workers of average ability had begun developing some bad work habits, becoming especially careless in her recordkeeping. After reprimand from the supervisor, the investigator corrected her errors and has been doing satisfactory work since then.
For the supervisor to keep referring to this period of poor work during her weekly conferences with this employee would generally be considered poor personnel practice CHIEFLY because
   A. praise rather than criticism is generally the best method to use in improving the work of an unsatisfactory worker
   B. the supervisor cannot know whether the employee's errors will follow an established pattern
   C. the fault which evoked the original negative criticism no longer exists
   D. this would tend to frustrate the worker by making her strive overly hard to reach a level of productivity which is beyond her ability to achieve

23.____

24. Assume that you are now a supervisor in a specific unit. Two experienced investigators in your unit, both of whom do above average work, have for some time not gotten along with each other for personal reasons Their attitude toward one another has suddenly become hostile and noisy disagreement has taken place in the office.
The BEST action for you to take FIRST in this situation is to
   A. transfer one of the two investigators to another unit where contact with the other investigator will be unnecessary
   B. discuss the problem with the two investigators together, insisting that they confide in you and tell you the cause of their mutual antagonism
   C. confer with the two investigators separately, pointing out to each the need to adopt an adult professional attitude with respect to their on-the-job relations
   D. advise the two investigators that should the situation grow worse, disciplinary action will be considered

24.____

25. It has long been recognized that relationships exist between worker morale and working conditions.
The one of the following which BEST clarifies these existing relationships is that morale is
   A. affected for better or worse in direct relationship to the magnitude of the changes in working conditions for better or worse
   B. better when working conditions are better
   C. little affected by working conditions so long as the working conditions do not approach the intolerable
   D. more affected by the degree of interest shown in providing good working conditions than by the actual conditions and may, perversely, be highest when working conditions are worst

KEY (CORRECT ANSWERS)

1.	A	11.	D
2.	D	12.	A
3.	B	13.	C
4.	A	14.	D
5.	D	15.	A
6.	D	16.	D
7.	B	17.	A
8.	C	18.	A
9.	A	19.	B
10.	C	20.	B

21. A
22. D
23. C
24. C
25. D

EXAMINATION SECTION
TEST 1

DIRECTIONS: Each question or incomplete statement is followed by several suggested answers or completions. Select the one that BEST answers the question or completes the statement. *PRINT THE LETTER OF THE CORRECT ANSWER IN THE SPACE AT THE RIGHT.*

1. Which one of the following is LEAST likely to be an area or cause of trouble in the use of staff personnel?

    A. Misunderstanding of the role the staff personnel are supposed to play as a result of vagueness of definition of their duties and authority
    B. Tendency of staff personnel almost always to be older than line personnel at comparable salary levels with whom they must deal
    C. Selection of staff personnel who fail to have simultaneously both competence in their specialities and skill in staff work
    D. The staff person fails to understand mixed staff and operating duties

2. Which of the following is generally NOT a valid statement with respect to the supervisory process?

    A. General supervision is more effective than close supervision.
    B. Employee-centered supervisors lead more effectively than do production-centered supervisors.
    C. Employee satisfaction is directly related to productivity.
    D. Low-producing supervisors use techniques that are different from high-producing supervisors.

3. Which of the following is the MOST essential element for proper evaluation of the performance of subordinate supervisors?

    A. Careful definition of each supervisor's specific job responsibilities and of his progress in meeting mutually agreed upon work goals
    B. System of rewards and penalties based on each supervisor's progress in meeting clearly defined performance standards
    C. Definition of personality traits, such as industry, initiative, dependability, and cooperativeness, required for effective job performance
    D. Breakdown of each supervisor's job into separate components and a rating of his performance on each individual task

4. The PRINCIPAL advantage of specialization for the operating efficiency of a public service agency is that specialization

    A. reduces the amount of red tape in coordinating the activities of mutually dependent departments
    B. simplifies the problem of developing adequate job controls
    C. provides employees with a clear understanding of the relationship of their activities to the overall objectives of the agency
    D. reduces destructive competition for power between departments

5. A list of conditions which encourages good morale inside a work group would NOT include a

   A. high rate of agreement among group members on values and objectives
   B. tight control system to minimize the risk of individual error
   C. good possibility that joint action will accomplish goals
   D. past history of successful group accomplishment

6. Of the following, the MOST important factor to be considered in selecting a training strategy or program is the

   A. requirements of the job to be performed by the trainees
   B. educational level or prior training of the trainees
   C. size of the training group
   D. quality and competence of available training specialists

7. Of the following, the one which is considered to be LEAST characteristic of the higher ranks of management is

   A. that higher levels of management benefit from modern technology
   B. that success is measured by the extent to which objectives are achieved
   C. the number of subordinates that directly report to a manager
   D. the de-emphasis of individual and specialized performance

8. Assume that a manager is preparing a training syllabus to be used in training members of her staff.
   Which of the following would NOT be a valid principle of the learning process to consider when preparing this training syllabus?

   A. When a person has thoroughly learned a task, it takes a lot of effort to create a little more improvement.
   B. In complicated learning situations, there is a period in which an additional period of practice produces an equal amount of improvement in learning.
   C. The less a person knows about the task, the slower the initial progress.
   D. The more a person knows about the task, the slower the initial progress.

9. Which statement BEST illustrates when collective bargaining agreements are working well?

   A. Executives strongly support subordinate managers.
   B. The management rights clause in the contract is clear and enforced.
   C. Contract provisions are competently interpreted.
   D. The provisions of the agreement are properly interpreted, communicated, and observed.

10. An executive who wishes to encourage subordinates to communicate freely with him about a job-related problem should FIRST

   A. state his own position on the problem before listening to the subordinates' ideas
   B. invite subordinates to give their own opinions on the problem
   C. ask subordinates for their reactions to his own ideas about the problem
   D. guard the confidentiality of management information about the problem

11. The ability to deal constructively with intra-organizational conflict is an essential attribute of the successful manager.
    The one of the following types of conflict which would be LEAST difficult to handle constructively is a situation in which there is

   A. agreement on objectives, but disagreement as to the probable results of adopting the various alternatives
   B. agreement on objectives, disagreement on alternative courses of action, and relative certainty as to the outcome of one of the alternatives
   C. disagreement on objectives and on alternative courses of action, and relative certainty as to the outcome of one of the alternatives
   D. disagreement on objectives and on alternative courses of action, but uncertainty as to the outcome of the alternatives

12. Which of the following actions does NOT belong in a properly conducted grievance handling process?

   A. Gathering relevant information on why the grievance arose
   B. Formulating a personal judgment about the fairness or unfairness of the grievance at the time the grievance is presented
   C. Establishing tentative answers to the grievance
   D. Following up to see whether the solution has eliminated the difficulty

13. Grievances are generally defined as complaints expressed over work-related matters.
    Which one of the following is MOST important for managers to be aware of in connection with this definition?
    The

   A. fact that the definition fails to separate the subject of the grievance from the attitude of the grievant
   B. fact that anything in the organization may be the source of the grievance
   C. need to assume that dissatisfied people have adverse effects on productivity
   D. implication that management should be concerned about expressed grievances and unconcerned about unexpressed grievances

14. In carrying out disciplinary action, the MOST important procedure for all managers to follow is to 14._____

    A. convince all levels of management on the need for discipline from the organization's viewpoint
    B. follow up on a disciplinary action and not assume that the action has been effective
    C. convince all executives that proper discipline is a legitimate tool for their use
    D. convince all executives that they need to display confidence in the organization's rules

15. Assume that an employee under your supervision is acquitted in court of criminal charges arising out of his employment. 15._____
    Of the following statements concerning disciplinary action, which is MOST NEARLY correct?

    A. Disciplinary proceedings against the employee may not be held for the same offenses on which he was tried and acquitted.
    B. In a disciplinary action, the acquittal dispenses with the requirement that the employee be advised as to his constitutional rights.
    C. Civil Rights Law Section 79 prohibits the taking of any further punitive action by an employer if the offense did not involve official corruption.
    D. It is possible for the employee to be found guilty of the same offense when tried in a departmental hearing.

16. Work rules can be an effective tool in the process of personnel management. 16._____
    The BEST practical definition for work rules is that they are

    A. minimum standards of conduct or performance that apply to individuals or groups at work in an organization
    B. prescriptions that serve to specialize employee behavior
    C. predetermined decisions about disciplinary action
    D. the major determinant of an organization's climate and the morale of its workforce

Questions 17-18

DIRECTIONS: Questions 17 and 18 pertain to identification of words that are incorrectly used because they are not in keeping with the meaning of the quotation. In answering each question, the first step is to read the passage and identify the incorrectly used word, and then select the word which, when substituted, BEST serves to convey the meaning of the quotation.

17. Among the Housing Manager's overall responsibilities in administering a project is the prevention of the development of conditions which might lead to termination of tenancy and eviction of a tenant. Where there appears to be doubt that a tenant is fully aware of his responsibilities and is thus jeopardizing his tenancy, the Housing Manager should acquaint him with these responsibilities. Where a situation involves behavior of a tenant or a member of his family, the Housing Manager should confirm, through discussions and referrals to social agencies, correction of the conditions before they reach a state where there is no alternative but termination proceedings.

    A. Coordinate
    B. Identify
    C. Assert
    D. Attempt

    17._____

18. The one universal administrative complaint is that the budget is inadequate. Between adequacy and inadequacy lie all degrees of adequacy. Further, human wants are modest in relation to human resources. From these two facts we may conclude that the fundamental criterion of administrative decision must be a criterion of efficiency (the degree to which the goals have been reached relative to the available resources) rather than a criterion of adequacy (the degree to which its goals have been reached). The task of the manager is to maximize social values relative to limited resources.

    A. Improve
    B. Simple
    C. Limitless
    D. Optimize

    18._____

Questions 19-21.
DIRECTIONS: Questions 19 through 21 are to be answered SOLELY on the basis of the following situation.

John Foley, a top administrator, is responsible for output in his organization. Because productivity had been lagging for two periods in a row, Foley decided to establish a committee of his subordinate managers to investigate the reasons for the poor performance and to make recommendations for improvements. After two meetings, the committee came to the conclusions and made the recommendations that follow.

Output forecasts had been handed down from the top without prior consultation with middle management and first level supervision. Lines of authority and responsibility had been unclear. The planning and control process should be decentralized.

After receiving the committee's recommendations, Foley proceeded to take the following actions. Foley decided he would retain final authority to establish quotas but would delegate to the middle managers the responsibility for meeting quotas.

After receiving Foley's decision, the middle managers proceeded to delegate to the first-line supervisors the authority to establish their own quotas. The middle managers eventually received and combined the first-line supervisors' quotas so that these conformed to Foley's.

19. Foley's decision to delegate responsibility for meeting quotas to the middle managers is inconsistent with sound management principles because

    A. Foley should not have involved himself in the first place
    B. middle managers do not have the necessary skills
    C. quotas should be established by the chief executive
    D. responsibility should not be delegated

20. The principle of co-extensiveness of responsibility and authority bears on Foley's decision.
    In this case, it implies that

    A. authority should exceed responsibility
    B. authority should be delegated to match the degree of responsibility
    C. both authority and responsibility should be retained and not delegated
    D. responsibility should be delegated, but authority should be retained

21. The middle managers' decision to delegate to the first-line supervisors the authority to establish quotas was INCORRECTLY reasoned because

    A. delegation and control must go together
    B. first-line supervisors are in no position to establish quotas
    C. one cannot delegate authority that one does not possess
    D. the meeting of quotas should not be delegated

22. If one attempts to list the advantages of the management-by-exception principle as it is used in connection with the budgeting process, several distinct advantages could be cited.
    Which of the following is NOT an advantage of this principle as it applies to the budgeting process?
    Management-by-exception

    A. saves time
    B. identifies critical problem areas
    C. focuses attention and concentrates effort
    D. escalates the frequency and importance of budget-related decisions

23. The MOST accurate description of a budget is that

    A. a budget is made up by an organization to plan its future activities
    B. a budget specifies in dollars and cents how much is spent in a particular time period
    C. a budget specifies how much the organization to which it relates estimates it will spend over a certain period of time
    D. all plans dealing with money are budgets

24. Of the following, the one which is NOT a contribution that a budget makes to organizational programming is that a budget

   A. enables a comparison of what actually happened with what was expected
   B. stresses the need to forecast specific goals and eliminates the need to focus on tasks needed to accomplish goals
   C. may illustrate duplication of effort between interdependent activities
   D. shows the relationship between various organizational segments

24._____

25. A line-item budget is a good control budget because

   A. it clearly specifies how the items being purchased will be used
   B. expenditures can be shown primarily for contractual services
   C. it clearly specifies what the money is buying
   D. it clearly specifies the services to be provided

25._____

KEY (CORRECT ANSWERS)

1.	B	11.	B
2.	C	12.	B
3.	A	13.	C
4.	B	14.	B
5.	B	15.	D
6.	A	16.	A
7.	A	17.	D
8.	D	18.	C
9.	D	19.	D
10.	B	20.	B

21.	C
22.	D
23.	C
24.	B
25.	C

TEST 2

DIRECTIONS: Each question or incomplete statement is followed by several suggested answers or completions. Select the one that BEST answers the question or completes the statement. *PRINT THE LETTER OF THE CORRECT ANSWER IN THE SPACE AT THE RIGHT.*

1. The insights of Chester I. Barnard have influenced the development of management thought in significant ways. He is MOST closely identified with a position that has become known as the

    A. acceptance theory of authority
    B. principle of the manager's or executive's span of control
    C. *Theory X* and *Theory Y* dichotomy
    D. unit of command principle

    1._____

2. Certain conditions should exist to insure that a subordinate will decide to accept a communication as being authoritative.
Which of the following is LEAST valid as a condition which should exist?

    A. The subordinate understands the communication.
    B. At the time of the subordinate's decision, he views the communication as consistent with the organization's purpose and his personal interest.
    C. At the time of the subordinate's decision, he views the communication as more consistent with his personal purposes than with the organization's interest.
    D. The subordinate is mentally and physically able to comply with the communication.

    2._____

3. In exploring the effects that employee participation has on implementing changes in work methods, certain relationships have been established between participation and productivity.
It has MOST generally been found that highest productivity occurs in groups provided with

    A. participation in the process of change only through representatives of their group
    B. no participation in the change process
    C. full participation in the change process
    D. intermittent participation in the process of change

    3._____

4. The trend LEAST likely to occur in the area of employee-management relations is that

    A. employees will exert more influence on decisions affecting their interests
    B. technological change will have a stronger impact on organizations' human resources
    C. labor will judge management according to company profits
    D. government will play a larger role in balancing the interests of the parties in labor-management affairs

    4._____

5. Members of an organization must satisfy several fundamental psychological needs in order to be happy and productive.
The BROADEST and MOST basic needs are

    A. achievement, recognition, and acceptance
    B. competition, recognition, and accomplishment
    C. salary increments and recognition
    D. acceptance of competition and economic award

6. Morale has been defined as the capacity of a group of people to pull together steadily for a common purpose.
Morale thus defined is MOST generally dependent on

    A. job security
    B. group and individual self-confidence
    C. organizational efficiency
    D. physical health of the individuals

7. Which is the CORRECT order of steps to follow when revising office procedure?
To

    I. develop the improved method as determined by time and motion studies and effective workplace layout
    II. find out how the task is now performed
    III. apply the new method
    IV. analyze the current method

    The CORRECT answer is:
    A. IV, II, I, III   B. II, I, III, IV
    C. I, II, IV, III   D. II, IV, I, III

8. In contrast to broad spans of control, narrow spans of control are MOST likely to

    A. provide opportunity for more personal contact between superior and subordinate
    B. encourage decentralization
    C. stress individual initiative
    D. foster group of team effort

9. A manager is coaching a subordinate on the nature of decision-making. She could BEST define decision-making as

    A. choosing between alternatives
    B. making diagnoses of feasible ends
    C. making diagnoses of feasible means
    D. comparing alternatives

10. Of the following, the LEAST valid purpose of an organizational policy statement is to

    A. keep personnel from performing improper actions and functions on routine matters
    B. prevent the mishandling of non-routine matters
    C. provide management personnel with a tool that precludes the need for their use of judgment
    D. provide standard decisions and approaches in handling problems of a recurrent nature

11. Current thinking on bureaucratic organizations is that

    A. bureaucracy is on the way out
    B. bureaucracy, though not perfect, is unlikely to be replaced
    C. bureaucratic organizations are most effective in dealing with constant change
    D. bureaucratic organizations are most effective when dealing with sophisticated customers or clients

12. The development of alternate plans as a major step in planning will normally result in the planner's having several possible course of action available. GENERALLY, this is

    A. *desirable* since such development helps to determine the most suitable alternative and to provide for the unexpected
    B. *desirable* since such development makes the use of planning premises and constraints unnecessary
    C. *undesirable* since the planners should formulate only one way of achieving given goals at a given time
    D. *undesirable* since such action restricts efforts to modify the planning to take advantage of opportunities

13. Assume a manager carries out his responsibilities to his staff according to what is now known about managerial leadership.
    Which of the following statements would MOST accurately reflect his assumptions about proper management?

    A. Efficiency in operations results from allowing the human element to participate in a minimal way.
    B. Efficient operation results from balancing work considerations with personnel considerations.
    C. Efficient operation results from a work force committed to its self-interest.
    D. Efficient operation results from staff relationships that produce a friendly work climate.

14. Assume that a manager is called upon to conduct a management audit. To do this properly, he would have to take certain steps in a specific sequence. Which step should this manager take FIRST?

    A. Managerial performance must be surveyed.
    B. A method of reporting must be established.
    C. Management auditing procedures and documentation must be developed.
    D. Criteria for the audit must be established.

14._____

15. If a manager is required to conduct a scientific investigation of an organizational problem, the FIRST step he should take is to

    A. state his assumptions about the problem
    B. carry out a search for background information
    C. choose the right approach to investigate the validity of his assumptions
    D. define and state the problem

15._____

16. A manager would be correct to assert that the principle of delegation states that decisions should be made PRIMARILY

    A. by persons in an executive capacity qualified to make them
    B. by persons in a non-executive capacity
    C. at as low an organizational level of authority as practicable
    D. by the next lower level of authority

16._____

17. Of the following, which one is NOT regarded by management authorities as a fundamental characteristic of an ideal bureaucracy?

    A. Division of labor and specialization
    B. An established hierarchy
    C. Decentralization of authority
    D. A set of operating rules and regulations

17._____

18. As the number of subordinates in a manager's span of control increases, the actual number of possible relationships

    A. increases disproportionately to the number of subordinates
    B. increases in equal number to the number of subordinates
    C. reaches a stable level
    D. will first increase, then slowly decrease

18._____

19. Management experts generally believe that computer-based management information systems (MIS) have greater potential for improving the process of management than any other development in recent decades.
    The one of the following which MOST accurately describes the objectives of MIS is to

    A. provide information for decision-making on planning, initiating, and controlling the operations of the various units of the organization
    B. establish mechanization of routine functions such as clerical records, payroll, inventory, and accounts receivable in order to promote economy and efficiency
    C. computerize decision-making on planning, initiating, organizing, and controlling the operations of an organization
    D. provide accurate facts and figures on the various programs of the organization to be used for purposes of planning and research

20. The one of the following which is the BEST application of the *management-by-exception* principle is that this principle

    A. stimulates communication and aids in management of crisis situations, thus reducing the frequency of decision-making
    B. saves time and reserves top management decisions only for crisis situations, thus reducing the frequency of decision-making
    C. stimulates communication, saves time, and reduces the frequency of decision-making
    D. is limited to crisis-management situations

21. Generally, each organization is dependent upon the availability of qualified personnel.
    Of the following, the MOST important factor affecting the availability of qualified people to each organization is

    A. availability of public transportation
    B. the general rise in the educational levels of our population
    C. the rise of sentiment against racial discrimination
    D. pressure by organized community groups

22. A fundamental responsibility of all managers is to decide what physical facilities and equipment are needed to help attain basic goals.
    Good planning for the purchase and use of equipment is seldom easy to do and is complicated most by the fact that

    A. organizations rarely have stable sources of supply
    B. nearly all managers tend to be better at personnel planning than at equipment planning
    C. decisions concerning physical resources are made too often on an emergency basis rather than under carefully prepared policies
    D. legal rulings relative to depreciation fluctuate very frequently

23. In attempting to reconcile managerial objectives and an individual employee's goals, it is generally LEAST desirable for management to

    A. recognize the capacity of the individual to contribute toward realization of managerial goals
    B. encourage self-development of the employee to exceed minimum job performance
    C. consider an individual employee's work separately from other employees
    D. demonstrate that an employee advances only to the extent that he contributes directly to the accomplishment of stated goals

24. As a management tool for discovering individual training needs, a job analysis would generally be of LEAST assistance in determining

    A. the performance requirements of individual jobs
    B. actual employee performance on the job
    C. acceptable standards of performance
    D. training needs for individual jobs

25. One of the major concerns of organizational managers today is how the spread of automation will affect them and the status of their positions. Realistically speaking, one can say that the MOST likely effect of our newer forms of highly automated technology on managers will be to

    A. make most top-level positions superfluous or obsolete
    B. reduce the importance of managerial work in general
    C. replace the work of managers with the work of technicians
    D. increase the importance of and demand for top managerial personnel

KEY (CORRECT ANSWERS)

1. A	11. B
2. C	12. A
3. C	13. B
4. C	14. D
5. A	15. D
6. B	16. C
7. D	17. C
8. A	18. A
9. A	19. A
10. C	20. C

21. B
22. C
23. C
24. B
25. D

REPORT WRITING
EXAMINATION SECTION
TEST 1

DIRECTIONS: Each question or incomplete statement is followed by several suggested answers or completions. Select the one that BEST answers the question or completes the statement. *PRINT THE LETTER OF THE CORRECT ANSWER IN THE SPACE AT THE RIGHT.*

Questions 1-3.

DIRECTIONS: Questions 1 to 3 are based on the following example of a report. The report consists of ten numbered sentences, some of which are *not* consistent with the principles of good report writing.

(1) On the evening of February 24, Roscoe and Leroy, two members of the "Red Devils," were entering with a bottle of wine in their hands. (2) It was unusually good wine for these boys to buy, (3) I told them to give me the bottle and they refused, and added that they wouldn't let anyone "put them out." (4) I told them they were entitled to have a good time, but they could not do it the way they wanted; there were certain rules they had to observe. (5) At this point, Roscoe said he had seen me box at camp and suggested that Leroy not accept my offer. (6) Then I said firmly that the admission fee did not give them the authority to tell me what to do. (7) I also told them that, if they thought I would fight them over such a matter, they were sadly mistaken. (8) I added, however, that we could go to the gym right now and settle it another way if they wished. (9) Leroy immediately said that he was sorry, he had not understood the rules, and he did not want his quarter back. (10) On the other hand, they would not give up their bottle either, so they left the premises.

1. Only material that is relevant to the main thought of a report should be included. Which of the following sentences from the report contains material which is LEAST relevant to this report? Sentence
   "A. 2   B. 3   C. 8   D. 9

1.____

2. A good report should be arranged in logical order. Which of the following sentences from the report does NOT appear in its proper sequence in the report? Sentence
   A. 3   B. 5   C. 7   D. 9

2.____

3. Reports should include all essential information. Of the following, the MOST important fact that is *missing* from this report is:
   A. Who was involved in the incident   B. How the incident was resolved
   C. When the incident took place   D. Where the incident took place

3.____

4. The MOST serious of the following faults *commonly* found in explanatory reports is
   A. the use of slang terms   B. excessive details
   C. personal bias   D. redundancy

4.____

109

5. In reviewing a report he has prepared to submit to his superiors, a supervisor finds that his paragraphs are a typewritten page long and decides to make some revisions.
Of the following, the MOST important question he should ask about each paragraph is
   A. Are the words too lengthy?
   B. Is the idea under discussion too abstract?
   C. Is more than one central thought being expressed?
   D. Are the sentences too long?

6. The summary or findings of a long management report intended for the typical manager should, *generally*, appear _____ the report.
   A. at the very beginning of
   B. at the end of
   C. throughout
   D. in the middle of

7. In preparing a report that includes several tables, if not otherwise instructed, the typist should MOST properly include a list of tables
   A. in the introductory part of the report
   B. at the end of each chapter in the body of the report
   C. in the supplementary part of the report as an appendix
   D. in the supplementary part of the report as a part of the index

8. When typing a preliminary draft of a report, the one of the following which you should *generally* NOT do is to
   A. erase typing errors and deletions rather than "X"ing them out
   B. leave plenty of room at the top, bottom, and sides of each page
   C. make only the number of copies that you are asked to make
   D. type double or triple space

9. When you determine the methods of emphasis you will use in typing the titles, headings and subheadings of a report, the one of the following which it is MOST important to keep in mind is that
   A. all headings of the same rank should be typed in the same way
   B. all headings should be typed in the single style which is most pleasing to the eye
   C. headings should not take up more than one-third of the page width
   D. only one method should be used for all headings, whatever their rank

10. The one of the following ways in which inter-office memoranda *differ* from long formal reports is that they, *generally*,
    A. are written as if the reader is familiar with the vocabulary and technical background of the writer
    B. do not have a "subject line" which describes the major topic covered in the text
    C. include a listing of reference materials which support the memo writer's conclusions
    D. require that a letter of transmittal be attached

11. It is *preferable* to print information on a field report rather than write it out longhand MAINLY because
    A. printing takes less time to write than writing long hand
    B. printing is usually easier to read than longhand writing
    C. longhand writing on field reports is not acceptable in court cases
    D. printing occupies less space on a report than longhand writing

12. Of the following characteristics of a written report, the one that is MOST important is its
    A. length   B. accuracy   C. organization   D. grammar

13. A written report to your superior contains many spelling errors.
    Of the following statements relating to spelling errors, the one that is MOST NEARLY correct is that
    A. this is unimportant as long as the meaning of the report is clear
    B. readers of the report will ignore the many spelling errors
    C. readers of the report will get a poor opinion of the writer of the report
    D. spelling errors are unimportant as long as the grammar is correct

14. Written reports to your superior should have the same general arrangement and layout.
    The BEST reason for this requirement is that the
    A. report will be more accurate
    B. report will be more complete
    C. person who reads the report will know what the subject of the report is
    D. person who reads the report will know where to look for information in the report

15. The first paragraph of a report usually contains detailed information on the subject of the report.
    Of the following, the BEST reason for this requirement is to enable the
    A. reader to quickly find the subject of the report
    B. typist to immediately determine the subject of the report so that she will understand what she is typing
    C. clerk to determine to whom copies of the report will be needed
    D. typist to quickly determine how many copies of the report will be needed

16. Of the following statements concerning reports, the one which is LEAST valid is:
    A. A case report should contain factual material to support conclusions made
    B. An extremely detailed report may be of less value than a brief report giving the essential facts
    C. Highly technical language should be avoided as far as possible in preparing a report to be used at a court trial
    D. The position of the important facts in a report does not influence the emphasis placed on them by the reader

17. Suppose that you realize that you have made an error in a report that has been forwarded to another unit. You know that this error is not likely to be discovered for some time.
Of the following, the MOST advisable course of action for you to take is to
    A. approach the supervisor of the other unit on an informal basis, and ask him to correct the error
    B. say nothing about it since most likely one error will not invalidate the entire report
    C. tell your supervisor immediately that you have made an error so that it may be corrected, if necessary
    D. wait until the error is discovered and then admit that you had made it

18. In a report, words in a sentence must be arranged properly to make sure that the intended meaning of the sentence is clear.
The sentence below that does NOT make sense because a clause has been separated from the word on which its meaning depends is:
    A. To be a good writer, clarity is necessary.
    B. To be a good writer, you must write clearly.
    C. You must write clearly to be a good writer.
    D. Clarity is necessary to good writing.

19. The use of a graph to show statistical data in a report is *superior* to a table because it
    A. emphasizes approximations
    B. emphasizes facts and relationships more dramatically
    C. presents data more accurately
    D. is easily understood by the average reader

20. Of the following, the degree of formality required of a written report is, MOST likely to depend on the
    A. subject matter of the report
    B. frequency of its occurrence
    C. amount of time available for its preparation
    D. audience for whom the report is intended

Questions 21-25.

DIRECTIONS: Questions 21 through 25 consist of sets of four sentences lettered A, B, C, and D. For each question, choose the sentence which is grammatically and stylistically MOST appropriate for use in a formal written report.

21. A. It is recommended, therefore, that the impasse panel hearings are to be convened on September 30.
    B. It is therefore recommended that the impasse panel hearings be convened on September 30.
    C. Therefore, it is recommended to convene the impasse panel hearings on September 30.
    D. It is recommended that the impasse panel hearings therefore should be convened on September 30.

22. A. Penalties have been assessed for violating the Taylor Law by several unions.
    B. When they violated provisions of the Taylor Law, several unions were later penalized.
    C. Several unions have been penalized for violating provisions of the Taylor Law.
    D. Several unions' violating provisions of the Taylor Law resulted in them being penalized.

22.____

23. A. The number of disputes settled through mediation has increased significantly over the past two years.
    B. The number of disputes settled through mediation are increasing significantly over two-year periods.
    C. Over the past two years, through mediation, the number of disputes settled increased significantly.
    D. There is a significant increase over the past two years of the number of disputes settled through mediation.

23.____

24. A. The union members will vote to determine if the contract is to be approved.
    B. It is not yet known whether the union members will ratify the proposed contract.
    C. When the union members vote, that will determine the new contract.
    D. Whether the union members will ratify the proposed contract, it is not yet known.

24.____

25. A. The parties agreed to an increase in fringe benefits in return for greater work productivity.
    B. Greater productivity was agreed to be provided in return for increased fringe benefits.
    C. Productivity and fringe benefits are interrelated; the higher the former, the more the latter grows.
    D. The contract now provides that the amount of fringe benefits will depend upon the level of output by the workers.

25.____

KEY (CORRECT ANSWERS)

1. A
2. B
3. D
4. C
5. C

6. A
7. A
8. A
9. A
10. A

11. B
12. B
13. C
14. D
15. A

16. D
17. C
18. A
19. B
20. D

21. B
22. C
23. A
24. B
25. A

TEST 2

DIRECTIONS: Each question or incomplete statement is followed by several suggested answers or completions. Select the one that BEST answers the question or completes the statement. *PRINT THE LETTER OF THE CORRECT ANSWER IN THE SPACE AT THE RIGHT.*

Questions 1-4.

DIRECTIONS: Questions 1 through 4 are to be answered on the basis of the following report which was prepared by a supervisor for inclusion in his agency's annual report.

Line #

1   On Oct. 13, I was assigned to study the salaries paid
2   to clerical employees in various titles by the city and by
3   private industry in the area.
4   In order to get the data I needed, I called Mr. Johnson at
5   the Bureau of the Budget and the payroll officers at X Corp.-
6   a brokerage house, Y Co. –an insurance company, and Z Inc. –
7   a publishing firm. None of them was available and I had to call
8   all of them again the next day.
9   When I finally got the information I needed, I drew up a
10 chart, which is attached. Note that not all of the companies I
11 contacted employed people at all the different levels used in the
12 city service.
13 The conclusions I draw from analyzing this information is
14 as follows: The city's entry-level salary is about average for
15 the region; middle-level salaries are generally higher in the
16 city government than in private industry; but salaries at the
17 highest levels in private industry are better than city em-
18 ployees' pay.

1. Which of the following criticisms about the style in which this report is written is MOST valid?
   A. It is too informal.
   B. It is too concise.
   C. It is too choppy.
   D. The syntax is too complex.

2. Judging from the statements made in the report, the method followed by this employee in performing his research was
   A. *good*; he contacted a representative sample of businesses in the area
   B. *poor*; he should have drawn more definite conclusions
   C. *good*; he was persistent in collecting information
   D. *poor*; he did not make a thorough study

3. One sentence in this report contains a grammatical error. This sentence *begins* on line number
   A. 4   B. 7   C. 10   D. 13

4. The type of information given in this report which should be presented in footnotes or in an appendix, is the
   A. purpose of the study
   B. specifics about the businesses contacted
   C. reference to the chart
   D. conclusions drawn by the author

4._____

5. Of the following, a DISTINGUISHING characteristic of a written report intended for the head of your agency as compared to a report prepared for a lower-echilon staff member is that the report for the agency head should, *usually*, include
   A. considerably more detail, especially statistical data
   B. the essential details in an abbrevated form
   C. all available source material
   D. an annotated bibliography

5._____

6. Assume that you are asked to write a lengthy report for use by the administrator of your agency, the subject of which is "The Impact of Proposed New Data Processing Operations on Line Personnel" in your agency. You decide that the *most* appropriate type of report for you to prepare is an analytical report, including recommendations.
   The MAIN reason for your decision is that
   A. the subject of the report is extremely complex
   B. large sums of money are involved
   C. the report is being prepared for the administrator
   D. you intend to include charts and graphs

6._____

7. Assume that you are preparing a report based on a survey dealing with the attitudes of employees in Division X regarding proposed new changes in compensating employees for working overtime. Three percent of the respondents to the survey voluntarily offer an unfavorable opinion on the method of assigning overtime work, a question not specifically asked of the employees. On the basis of this information, the MOST appropriate and significant of the following comments for you to make in the report with regard to employees' attitudes on assigning overtime work is that
   A. an insignificant percentage of employees dislike the method of assigning overtime work
   B. three percent of the employees in Division X dislike the method of assigning overtime work
   C. three percent of the sample selected for the survey voiced an unfavorable opinion on the method of assigning overtime work
   D. some employees voluntarily voiced negative feelings about the method of assigning overtime work, making it impossible to determine the extent of this attitude

7._____

8. Assume that you have been asked to prepare a narrative summary of the monthly reports submitted by employees in your division.
   In preparing your summary of this month's reports, the FIRST step to take is to
   A. read through the reports, noting their general content and any unusual features
   B. decide how many typewritten pages your summary should contain
   C. make a written summary of each separate report, so that you will not have to go back to the original reports again
   D. ask each employee which points he would prefer to see emphasized in your summary

8._____

9. Assume that an administrative officer is writing a brief report to his superior outlining the advantages of matrix organization.
   Of the following, it would be INCORRECT to state that
   A. in matrix organization, a project is emphasized by designating one individual as the focal point for all matters pertaining to it
   B. utilization of manpower can be flexible in matrix organization because reservoir of specialists is maintained in the line operations
   C. the usual line-staff management is generally reversed in matrix organization
   D. in matrix organization, responsiveness to project needs is generally faster due to establishing needed communication lines and decision points

9._____

10. Written reports dealing with inspections of work and installations SHOULD be
    A. as long and detailed as practicable
    B. phrased with personal interpretations
    C. limited to the important facts of the inspection
    D. technically phrased to create an impression on superiors

10._____

11. It is important to use definite, exact words in preparing a descriptive report and to avoid, as much as possible, nouns that have vague meanings and, possibly, a different meaning for the reader than for the author.
    Which of the following sentences contains only nouns that are *definite* and *exact*?
    A. The free enterprise system should be vigorously encouraged in the United States.
    B. Arley Swopes climbed Mount Everest three times last year.
    C. Beauty is a characteristic of all the women at the party.
    D. Gil Noble asserts that he is a real democrat.

11._____

12. One way of shortening n unnecessarily long report is to reduce sentence length by eliminating the use of several words where a single one that does not alter the meaning will do.
    Which of the following sentences CANNOT be shortened without losing some of its information content?
    A. After being polished, the steel ball bearings ran at maximum speed.
    B. After the close of the war, John Taylor was made the recipient of a pension.
    C. In this day and age, you can call anyone up on the telephone.
    D. She is attractive in appearance, but she is a rather selfish person.

12._____

13. Employees are required to submit written reports of all unusual occurrences promptly.
    The BEST reason for such promptness is that the
    A. report may be too long if made at one's convenience
    C. report will tend to be more accurate as to facts
    D. employee is likely to make a better report under pressure

14. In making a report, it is poor practice to erase information on the report in order to make a change because
    A. there may be a question of what was changed and why it was changed
    B. you are likely to erase through the paper and tear the report
    C. the report will no longer look neat and presentable
    D. the duplicate copies will be smudged

15. The one of the following which BEST describes a periodic report is that it
    A. provides a record of accomplishments for a given time span and a comparison with similar time spans in the past
    B. covers the progress made in a project that has been postponed
    C. integrates, summarizes, and, perhaps, interprets published data on technical or scientific material
    D. describes a decision, advocates a policy or action, and presents facts in support of the writer's position

16. The PRIMARY purpose of including pictorial illustrations in a formal report is *usually* to
    A. amplify information which has been adequately treated verbally
    B. present details that are difficult to describe verbally
    C. provide the reader with a pleasant, momentary distraction
    D. present supplementary information incidental to the main ideas developed in the report

KEY (CORRECT ANSWERS)

1.	A		6.	A
2.	D		7.	D
3.	D		8.	A
4.	B		9.	C
5.	B		10.	C

11. B.
12. A.
13. C
14. A.
15. A.
16. B.

PHILOSOPHY, PRINCIPLES, PRACTICES, AND TECHNICS OF SUPERVISION, ADMINISTRATION, MANAGEMENT, AND ORGANIZATION

TABLE OF CONTENTS

	Page
MEANING OF SUPERVISION	1
THE OLD AND THE NEW SUPERVISION	1
THE EIGHT (8) BASIC PRINCIPLES OF THE NEW SUPERVISION	1
I. Principle of Responsibility	1
II. Principle of Authority	2
III. Principle of Self-Growth	2
IV. Principle of Individual Worth	2
V. Principle of Creative Leadership	2
VI. Principle of Success and Failure	2
VII. Principle of Science	3
VIII. Principle of Cooperation	3
WHAT IS ADMINISTRATION?	3
I. Practices Commonly Classed as "Supervisory"	3
II. Practices Commonly Classed as "Administrative"	3
III. Practices Commonly Classed as Both "Supervisory" and "Administrative"	4
RESPONSIBILITIES OF THE SUPERVISOR	4
COMPETENCIES OF THE SUPERVISOR	4
THE PROFESSIONAL SUPERVISOR-EMPLOYEE RELATIONSHIP	4
MINI-TEXT IN SUPERVISION, ADMINISTRATION, MANAGEMENT, AND ORGANIZATION	5
I. Brief Highlights	5
A. Levels of Management	6
B. What the Supervisor Must Learn	6
C. A Definition of Supervision	6
D. Elements of the Team Concept	6
E. Principles of Organization	6
F. The Four Important Parts of Every Job	7
G. Principles of Delegation	7
H. Principles of Effective Communications	7
I. Principles of Work Improvement	7
J. Areas of Job Improvement	7
K. Seven Key Points in Making Improvements	8

	L.	Corrective Techniques for Job Improvement	8
	M.	A Planning Checklist	8
	N.	Five Characteristics of Good Directions	9
	O.	Types of Directions	9
	P.	Controls	9
	Q.	Orienting the New Employee	9
	R.	Checklist for Orienting New Employees	9
	S.	Principles of Learning	10
	T.	Causes of Poor Performance	10
	U.	Four Major Steps in On-the-Job Instructions	10
	V.	Employees Want Five Things	10
	W.	Some Don'ts in Regard to Praise	11
	X.	How to Gain Your Workers' Confidence	11
	Y.	Sources of Employee Problems	11
	Z.	The Supervisor's Key to Discipline	11
	AA.	Five Important Processes of Management	12
	BB.	When the Supervisor Fails to Plan	12
	CC.	Fourteen General Principles of Management	12
	DD.	Change	12
II.	Brief Topical Summaries		13
	A.	Who/What is the Supervisor?	13
	B.	The Sociology of Work	13
	C.	Principles and Practices of Supervision	14
	D.	Dynamic Leadership	14
	E.	Processes for Solving Problems	15
	F.	Training for Results	15
	G.	Health, Safety, and Accident Prevention	16
	H.	Equal Employment Opportunity	16
	I.	Improving Communications	16
	J.	Self-Development	17
	K.	Teaching and Training	17
		1. The Teaching Process	17
		a. Preparation	17
		b. Presentation	18
		c. Summary	18
		d. Application	18
		e. Evaluation	18
		2. Teaching Methods	18
		a. Lecture	18
		b. Discussion	18
		c. Demonstration	19
		d. Performance	19
		e. Which Method to Use	19

PHILOSOPHY, PRINCIPLES, PRACTICES, AND TECHNICS
OF
SUPERVISION, ADMINISTRATION, MANAGEMENT, AND ORGANIZATION

MEANING OF SUPERVISION

The extension of the democratic philosophy has been accompanied by an extension in the scope of supervision. Modern leaders and supervisors no longer think of supervision in the narrow sense of being confined chiefly to visiting employees, supplying materials, or rating the staff. They regard supervision as being intimately related to all the concerned agencies of society, they speak of the supervisor's function in terms of "growth," rather than the "improvement" of employees.

This modern concept of supervision may be defined as follows: Supervision is leadership and the development of leadership within groups which are cooperatively engaged in inspection, research, training, guidance, and evaluation.

THE OLD AND THE NEW SUPERVISION

TRADITIONAL
1. Inspection
2. Focused on the employee
3. Visitation
4. Random and haphazard
5. Imposed and authoritarian
6. One person usually

MODERN
1. Study and analysis
2. Focused on aims, materials, methods, supervisors, employees, environment
3. Demonstrations, intervisitation, workshops, directed reading, bulletins, etc.
4. Definitely organized and planned (scientific)
5. Cooperative and democratic
6. Many persons involved (creative)

THE EIGHT (8) BASIC PRINCIPLES OF THE NEW SUPERVISION

I. Principle of Responsibility
   Authority to act and responsibility for acting must be joined.
   A. If you give responsibility, give authority.
   B. Define employee duties clearly.
   C. Protect employees from criticism by others.
   D. Recognize the rights as well as obligations of employees.
   E. Achieve the aims of a democratic society insofar as it is possible within the area of your work.
   F. Establish a situation favorable to training and learning.
   G. Accept ultimate responsibility for everything done in your section, unit, office, division, department.
   H. Good administration and good supervision are inseparable.

II. Principle of Authority
The success of the supervisor is measured by the extent to which the power of authority is not used.
   A. Exercise simplicity and informality in supervision
   B. Use the simplest machinery of supervision
   C. If it is good for the organization as a whole, it is probably justified.
   D. Seldom be arbitrary or authoritative.
   E. Do not base your work on the power of position or of personality.
   F. Permit and encourage the free expression of opinions.

III. Principle of Self-Growth
The success of the supervisor is measured by the extent to which, and the speed with which, he is no longer needed.
   A. Base criticism on principles, not on specifics.
   B. Point out higher activities to employees.
   C. Train for self-thinking by employees to meet new situations.
   D. Stimulate initiative, self-reliance, and individual responsibility
   E. Concentrate on stimulating the growth of employees rather than on removing defects.

IV. Principle of Individual Worth
Respect for the individual is a paramount consideration in supervision.
   A. Be human and sympathetic in dealing with employees.
   B. Don't nag about things to be done.
   C. Recognize the individual differences among employees and seek opportunities to permit best expression of each personality.

V. Principle of Creative Leadership
The best supervision is that which is not apparent to the employee.
   A. Stimulate, don't drive employees to creative action.
   B. Emphasize doing good things.
   C. Encourage employees to do what they do best.
   D. Do not be too greatly concerned with details of subject or method.
   E. Do not be concerned exclusively with immediate problems and activities.
   F. Reveal higher activities and make them both desired and maximally possible.
   G. Determine procedures in the light of each situation but see that these are derived from a sound basic philosophy.
   H. Aid, inspire, and lead so as to liberate the creative spirit latent in all good employees.

VI. Principle of Success and Failure
There are no unsuccessful employees, only unsuccessful supervisors who have failed to give proper leadership.
   A. Adapt suggestions to the capacities, attitudes, and prejudices of employees.
   B. Be gradual, be progressive, be persistent.
   C. Help the employee find the general principle; have the employee apply his own problem to the general principle.
   D. Give adequate appreciation for good work and honest effort.
   E. Anticipate employee difficulties and help to prevent them.
   F. Encourage employees to do the desirable things they will do anyway.
   G. Judge your supervision by the results it secures.

VII. Principle of Science
Successful supervision is scientific, objective, and experimental. It is based on facts, not on prejudices.
- A. Be cumulative in results.
- B. Never divorce your suggestions from the goals of training.
- C. Don't be impatient of results.
- D. Keep all matters on a professional, not a personal, level.
- E. Do not be concerned exclusively with immediate problems and activities.
- F. Use objective means of determining achievement and rating where possible.

VIII. Principle of Cooperation
Supervision is a cooperative enterprise between supervisor and employee.
- A. Begin with conditions as they are.
- B. Ask opinions of all involved when formulating policies.
- C. Organization is as good as its weakest link.
- D. Let employees help to determine policies and department programs.
- E. Be approachable and accessible—physically and mentally.
- F. Develop pleasant social relationships.

WHAT IS ADMINISTRATION

Administration is concerned with providing the environment, the material facilities, and the operational procedures that will promote the maximum growth and development of supervisors and employees. (Organization is an aspect and a concomitant of administration.)

There is no sharp line of demarcation between supervision and administration; these functions are intimately interrelated and, often, overlapping. They are complementary activities.

I. Practices Commonly Classed as "Supervisory"
- A. Conducting employees' conferences
- B. Visiting sections, units, offices, divisions, departments
- C. Arranging for demonstrations
- D. Examining plans
- E. Suggesting professional reading
- F. Interpreting bulletins
- G. Recommending in-service training courses
- H. Encouraging experimentation
- I. Appraising employee morale
- J. Providing for intervisitation

II. Practices Commonly Classified as "Administrative"
- A. Management of the office
- B. Arrangement of schedules for extra duties
- C. Assignment of rooms or areas
- D. Distribution of supplies
- E. Keeping records and reports
- F. Care of audio-visual materials
- G. Keeping inventory records
- H. Checking record cards and books

I. Programming special activities
  J. Checking on the attendance and punctuality of employees

III. Practices Commonly Classified as Both "Supervisory" and "Administrative"
  A. Program construction
  B. Testing or evaluating outcomes
  C. Personnel accounting
  D. Ordering instructional materials

RESPONSIBILITIES OF THE SUPERVISOR

A person employed in a supervisory capacity must constantly be able to improve his own efficiency and ability. He represent the employer to the employees and only continuous self-examination can make him a capable supervisor.

Leadership and training are the supervisor's responsibility. An efficient working unit is one in which the employees work with the supervisor. It is his job to bring out the best in his employees. He must always be relaxed, courteous, and calm in his association with his employees. Their feelings are important, and a harsh attitude does not develop the most efficient employees.

COMPETENCES OF THE SUPERVISOR

  I. Complete knowledge of the duties and responsibilities of his position.
  II. To be able to organize a job, plan ahead, and carry through.
  III. To have self-confidence and initiative.
  IV. To be able to handle the unexpected situation and make quick decisions.
  V. To be able to properly train subordinates in the positions they are best suited for.
  VI. To be able to keep good human relations among his subordinates.
  VII. To be able to keep good human relations between his subordinates and himself and to earn their respect and trust.

THE PROFESSIONAL SUPERVISOR-EMPLOYEE RELATIONSHIP

There are two kinds of efficiency: one kind is only apparent and is produced in organizations through the exercise of mere discipline; this is but a simulation of the second, or true, efficiency which springs from spontaneous cooperation. If you are a manager, no matter how great or small your responsibility, it is your job, in the final analysis, to create and develop this involuntary cooperation among the people whom you supervise. For, no matter how powerful a combination of money, machines, and materials a company may have, this is a dead and sterile thing without a team of willing, thinking, and articulate people to guide it.

The following 21 points are presented as indicative of the exemplary basic relationship that should exist between supervisor and employee:

1. Each person wants to be liked and respected by his fellow employee and wants to be treated with consideration and respect by his superior.
2. The most competent employee will make an error. However, in a unit where good relations exist between the supervisor and his employees, tenseness and fear do not exist. Thus, errors are not hidden or covered up, and the efficiency of a unit is not impaired.

3. Subordinates resent rules, regulations, or orders that are unreasonable or unexplained.
4. Subordinates are quick to resent unfairness, harshness, injustices, and favoritism.
5. An employee will accept responsibility if he knows that he will be complimented for a job well done, and not too harshly chastised for failure; that his supervisor will check the cause of the failure, and, if it was the supervisor's fault, he will assume the blame therefore. If it was the employee's fault, his supervisor will explain the correct method or means of handling the responsibility.
6. An employee wants to receive credit for a suggestion he has made, that is used. If a suggestion cannot be used, the employee is entitled to an explanation. The supervisor should not say "no" and close the subject.
7. Fear and worry slow up a worker's ability. Poor working environment can impair his physical and mental health. A good supervisor avoids forceful methods, threats, and arguments to get a job done.
8. A forceful supervisor is able to train his employees individually and as a team, and is able to motivate them in the proper channels.
9. A mature supervisor is able to properly evaluate his subordinates and to keep them happy and satisfied.
10. A sensitive supervisor will never patronize his subordinates.
11. A worthy supervisor will respect his employees' confidences.
12. Definite and clear-cut responsibilities should be assigned to each executive.
13. Responsibility should always be coupled with corresponding authority.
14. No change should be made in the scope or responsibilities of a position without a definite understanding to that effect on the part of all persons concerned.
15. No executive or employee, occupying a single position in the organization, should be subject to definite orders from more than one source.
16. Orders should never be given to subordinates over the head of a responsible executive. Rather than do this, the officer in question should be supplanted.
17. Criticisms of subordinates should, whoever possible, be made privately, and in no case should a subordinate be criticized in the presence of executives or employees of equal or lower rank.
18. No dispute or difference between executives or employees as to authority or responsibilities should be considered too trivial for prompt and careful adjudication.
19. Promotions, wage changes, and disciplinary action should always be approved by the executive immediately superior to the one directly responsible.
20. No executive or employee should ever be required, or expected, to be at the same time an assistant to, and critic of, another.
21. Any executive whose work is subject to regular inspection should, wherever practicable, be given the assistance and facilities necessary to enable him to maintain an independent check of the quality of his work.

MINI-TEXT IN SUPERVISION, ADMINISTRATION, MANAGEMENT, AND ORGANIZATION

I. Brief Highlights

Listed concisely and sequentially are major headings and important data in the field for quick recall and review.

A. Levels of Management
Any organization of some size has several levels of management. In terms of a ladder, the levels are:

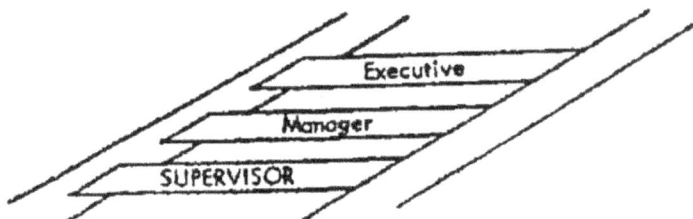

The first level is very important because it is the beginning point of management leadership.

B. What the Supervisor Must Learn
A supervisor must learn to:
1. Deal with people and their differences
2. Get the job done through people
3. Recognize the problems when they exist
4. Overcome obstacles to good performance
5. Evaluate the performance of people
6. Check his own performance in terms of accomplishment

C. A Definition of Supervisor
The term supervisor means any individual having authority, in the interests of the employer, to hire, transfer, suspend, lay-off, recall, promote, discharge, assign, reward, or discipline other employees or responsibility to direct them, or to adjust their grievances, or effectively to recommend such action, if, in connection with the foregoing, exercise of such authority is not of a merely routine or clerical nature but requires the use of independent judgment.

D. Elements of the Team Concept
What is involved in teamwork? The component parts are:
1. Members
2. A leader
3. Goals
4. Plans
5. Cooperation
6. Spirit

E. Principles of Organization
1. A team member must know what his job is.
2. Be sure that the nature and scope of a job are understood.
3. Authority and responsibility should be carefully spelled out.
4. A supervisor should be permitted to make the maximum number of decisions affecting his employees.
5. Employees should report to only one supervisor.
6. A supervisor should direct only as many employees as he can handle effectively.
7. An organization plan should be flexible.

8. Inspection and performance of work should be separate.
9. Organizational problems should receive immediate attention.
10. Assign work in line with ability and experience.

F. The Four Important Parts of Every Job
1. Inherent in every job is the *accountability* for results.
2. A second set of factors in every job is *responsibilities*.
3. Along with duties and responsibilities one must have the *authority* to act within certain limits without obtaining permission to proceed.
4. No job exists in a vacuum. The supervisor is surrounded by key *relationships*.

G. Principles of Delegation
Where work is delegated for the first time, the supervisor should think in terms of these questions:
1. Who is best qualified to do this?
2. Can an employee improve his abilities by doing this?
3. How long should an employee spend on this?
4. Are there any special problems for which he will need guidance?
5. How broad a delegation can I make?

H. Principles of Effective Communications
1. Determine the media.
2. To whom directed?
3. Identification and source authority.
4. Is communication understood?

I. Principles of Work Improvement
1. Most people usually do only the work which is assigned to them.
2. Workers are likely to fit assigned work into the time available to perform it.
3. A good workload usually stimulates output.
4. People usually do their best work when they know that results will be reviewed or inspected.
5. Employees usually feel that someone else is responsible for conditions of work, workplace layout, job methods, type of tools/equipment, and other such factors.
6. Employees are usually defensive about their job security.
7. Employees have natural resistance to change.
8. Employees can support or destroy a supervisor.
9. A supervisor usually earns the respect of his people through his personal example of diligence and efficiency.

J. Areas of Job Improvement
The areas of job improvement are quite numerous, but the most common ones which a supervisor can identify and utilize are:
1. Departmental layout
2. Flow of work
3. Workplace layout
4. Utilization of manpower
5. Work methods
6. Materials handling

7. Utilization
8. Motion economy

K. Seven Key Points in Making Improvements
1. Select the job to be improved
2. Study how it is being done now
3. Question the present method
4. Determine actions to be taken
5. Chart proposed method
6. Get approval and apply
7. Solicit worker participation

L. Corrective Techniques of Job Improvement
Specific Problems
1. Size of workload
2. Inability to meet schedules
3. Strain and fatigue
4. Improper use of men and skills
5. Waste, poor quality, unsafe conditions
6. Bottleneck conditions that hinder output
7. Poor utilization of equipment and machine
8. Efficiency and productivity of labor

General Improvement
1. Departmental layout
2. Flow of work
3. Work plan layout
4. Utilization of manpower
5. Work methods
6. Materials handling
7. Utilization of equipment
8. Motion economy

Corrective Techniques
1. Study with scale model
2. Flow chart study
3. Motion analysis
4. Comparison of units produced to standard allowance
5. Methods analysis
6. Flow chart and equipment study
7. Down time vs. running time
8. Motion analysis

M. A Planning Checklist
1. Objectives
2. Controls
3. Delegations
4. Communications
5. Resources
6. Manpower

7. Equipment
8. Supplies and materials
9. Utilization of time
10. Safety
11. Money
12. Work
13. Timing of improvements

N. Five Characteristics of Good Directions
In order to get results, directions must be:
1. Possible of accomplishment
2. Agreeable with worker interests
3. Related to mission
4. Planned and complete
5. Unmistakably clear

O. Types of Directions
1. Demands or direct orders
2. Requests
3. Suggestion or implication
4. volunteering

P. Controls
A typical listing of the overall areas in which the supervisor should establish controls might be:
1. Manpower
2. Materials
3. Quality of work
4. Quantity of work
5. Time
6. Space
7. Money
8. Methods

Q. Orienting the New Employee
1. Prepare for him
2. Welcome the new employee
3. Orientation for the job
4. Follow-up

R. Checklist for Orienting New Employees   Yes   No
1. Do you appreciate the feelings of new employees when they first report for work?   ___ ___
2. Are you aware of the fact that the new employee must make a big adjustment to his job?   ___ ___
3. Have you given him good reasons for liking the job and the organization?   ___ ___
4. Have you prepared for his first day on the job?   ___ ___
5. Did you welcome him cordially and make him feel needed?   ___ ___

	Yes	No

6. Did you establish rapport with him so that he feels free to talk and discuss matters with you? ___ ___
7. Did you explain his job to him and his relationship to you? ___ ___
8. Does he know that his work will be evaluated periodically on a basis that is fair and objective? ___ ___
9. Did you introduce him to his fellow workers in such a way that they are likely to accept him? ___ ___
10. Does he know what employee benefits he will receive? ___ ___
11. Does he understand the importance of being on the job and what to do if he must leave his duty station? ___ ___
12. Has he been impressed with the importance of accident prevention and safe practice? ___ ___
13. Does he generally know his way around the department? ___ ___
14. Is he under the guidance of a sponsor who will teach the right way of doing things? ___ ___
15. Do you plan to follow-up so that he will continue to adjust successfully to his job? ___ ___

S. Principles of Learning
   1. Motivation
   2. Demonstration or explanation
   3. Practice

T. Causes of Poor Performance
   1. Improper training for job
   2. Wrong tools
   3. Inadequate directions
   4. Lack of supervisory follow-up
   5. Poor communications
   6. Lack of standards of performance
   7. Wrong work habits
   8. Low morale
   9. Other

U. Four Major Steps in On-The-Job Instruction
   1. Prepare the worker
   2. Present the operation
   3. Tryout performance
   4. Follow-up

V. Employees Want Five Things
   1. Security
   2. Opportunity
   3. Recognition
   4. Inclusion
   5. Expression

W. Some Don'ts in Regard to Praise
1. Don't praise a person for something he hasn't done.
2. Don't praise a person unless you can be sincere.
3. Don't be sparing in praise just because your superior withholds it from you.
4. Don't let too much time elapse between good performance and recognition of it

X. How to Gain Your Workers' Confidence
Methods of developing confidence include such things as:
1. Knowing the interests, habits, hobbies of employees
2. Admitting your own inadequacies
3. Sharing and telling of confidence in others
4. Supporting people when they are in trouble
5. Delegating matters that can be well handled
6. Being frank and straightforward about problems and working conditions
7. Encouraging others to bring their problems to you
8. Taking action on problems which impede worker progress

Y. Sources of Employee Problems
On-the-job causes might be such things as:
1. A feeling that favoritism is exercised in assignments
2. Assignment of overtime
3. An undue amount of supervision
4. Changing methods or systems
5. Stealing of ideas or trade secrets
6. Lack of interest in job
7. Threat of reduction in force
8. Ignorance or lack of communications
9. Poor equipment
10. Lack of knowing how supervisor feels toward employee
11. Shift assignments

Off-the-job problems might have to do with:
1. Health
2. Finances
3. Housing
4. Family

Z. The Supervisor's Key to Discipline
There are several key points about discipline which the supervisor should keep in mind:
1. Job discipline is one of the disciplines of life and is directed by the supervisor.
2. It is more important to correct an employee fault than to fix blame for it.
3. Employee performance is affected by problems both on the job and off.
4. Sudden or abrupt changes in behavior can be indications of important employee problems.
5. Problems should be dealt with as soon as possible after they are identified.
6. The attitude of the supervisor may have more to do with solving problems than the techniques of problem solving.
7. Correction of employee behavior should be resorted to only after the supervisor is sure that training or counseling will not be helpful.

8. Be sure to document your disciplinary actions.
9. Make sure that you are disciplining on the basis of facts rather than personal feelings.
10. Take each disciplinary step in order, being careful not to make snap judgments, or decisions based on impatience.

AA. Five Important Processes of Management
1. Planning
2. Organizing
3. Scheduling
4. Controlling
5. Motivating

BB. When the Supervisor Fails to Plan
1. Supervisor creates impression of not knowing his job
2. May lead to excessive overtime
3. Job runs itself—supervisor lacks control
4. Deadlines and appointments missed
5. Parts of the work go undone
6. Work interrupted by emergencies
7. Sets a bad example
8. Uneven workload creates peaks and valleys
9. Too much time on minor details at expense of more important tasks

CC. Fourteen General Principles of Management
1. Division of work
2. Authority and responsibility
3. Discipline
4. Unity of command
5. Unity of direction
6. Subordination of individual interest to general interest
7. Remuneration of personnel
8. Centralization
9. Scalar chain
10. Order
11. Equity
12. Stability of tenure of personnel
13. Initiative
14. Esprit de corps

DD. Change

Bringing about change is perhaps attempted more often, and yet less well understood, than anything else the supervisor does. How do people generally react to change? (People tend to resist change that is imposed upon them by other individuals or circumstances.

Change is characteristic of every situation. It is a part of every real endeavor where the efforts of people are concerned.

1. Why do people resist change?
   People may resist change because of:
   a. Fear of the unknown
   b. Implied criticism
   c. Unpleasant experiences in the past
   d. Fear of loss of status
   e. Threat to the ego
   f. Fear of loss of economic stability

2. How can we best overcome the resistance to change?
   In initiating change, take these steps:
   a. Get ready to sell
   b. Identify sources of help
   c. Anticipate objections
   d. Sell benefits
   e. Listen in depth
   f. Follow up

II. Brief Topical Summaries

   A. Who/What is the Supervisor?
      1. The supervisor is often called the "highest level employee and the lowest level manager."
      2. A supervisor is a member of both management and the work group. He acts as a bridge between the two.
      3. Most problems in supervision are in the area of human relations, or people problems.
      4. Employees expect: Respect, opportunity to learn and to advance, and a sense of belonging, and so forth.
      5. Supervisors are responsible for directing people and organizing work. Planning is of paramount importance.
      6. A position description is a set of duties and responsibilities inherent to a given position.
      7. It is important to keep the position description up-to-date and to provide each employee with his own copy.

   B. The Sociology of Work
      1. People are alike in many ways; however, each individual is unique.
      2. The supervisor is challenged in getting to know employee differences. Acquiring skills in evaluating individuals is an asset.
      3. Maintaining meaningful working relationships in the organization is of great importance.
      4. The supervisor has an obligation to help individuals to develop to their fullest potential.
      5. Job rotation on a planned basis helps to build versatility and to maintain interest and enthusiasm in work groups.
      6. Cross training (job rotation) provides backup skills.

7. The supervisor can help reduce tension by maintaining a sense of humor, providing guidance to employees, and by making reasonable and timely decisions. Employees respond favorably to working under reasonably predictable circumstances.
8. Change is characteristic of all managerial behavior. The supervisor must adjust to changes in procedures, new methods, technological changes, and to a number of new and sometimes challenging situations.
9. To overcome the natural tendency for people to resist change, the supervisor should become more skillful in initiating change.

C. Principles and Practices of Supervision
1. Employees should be required to answer to only one superior.
2. A supervisor can effectively direct only a limited number of employees, depending upon the complexity, variety, and proximity of the jobs involved.
3. The organizational chart presents the organization in graphic form. It reflects lines of authority and responsibility as well as interrelationships of units within the organization.
4. Distribution of work can be improved through an analysis using the "Work Distribution Chart."
5. The "Work Distribution Chart" reflects the division of work within a unit in understandable form.
6. When related tasks are given to an employee, he has a better chance of increasing his skills through training.
7. The individual who is given the responsibility for tasks must also be given the appropriate authority to insure adequate results.
8. The supervisor should delegate repetitive, routine work. Preparation of recurring reports, maintaining leave and attendance records are some examples.
9. Good discipline is essential to good task performance. Discipline is reflected in the actions of employees on the job in the absence of supervision.
10. Disciplinary action may have to be taken when the positive aspects of discipline have failed. Reprimand, warning, and suspension are examples of disciplinary action.
11. If a situation calls for a reprimand, be sure it is deserved and remember it is to be done in private.

D. Dynamic Leadership
1. A style is a personal method or manner of exerting influence.
2. Authoritarian leaders often see themselves as the source of power and authority.
3. The democratic leader often perceives the group as the source of authority and power.
4. Supervisors tend to do better when using the pattern of leadership that is most natural for them.
5. Social scientists suggest that the effective supervisor use the leadership style that best fits the problem or circumstances involved.
6. All four styles—telling, selling, consulting, joining—have their place. Using one does not preclude using the other at another time.

7. The theory X point of view assumes that the average person dislikes work, will avoid it whenever possible, and must be coerced to achieve organizational objectives.
8. The theory Y point of view assumes that the average person considers work to be a natural as play, and, when the individual is committed, he requires little supervision or direction to accomplish desired objectives.
9. The leader's basic assumptions concerning human behavior and human nature affect his actions, decisions, and other managerial practices.
10. Dissatisfaction among employees is often present, but difficult to isolate. The supervisor should seek to weaken dissatisfaction by keeping promises, being sincere and considerate, keeping employees informed, and so forth.
11. Constructive suggestions should be encouraged during the natural progress of the work.

E. Processes for Solving Problems
1. People find their daily tasks more meaningful and satisfying when they can improve them.
2. The causes of problems, or the key factors, are often hidden in the background. Ability to solve problems often involves the ability to isolate them from their backgrounds. There is some substance to the cliché that some persons "can't see the forest for the trees."
3. New procedures are often developed from old ones. Problems should be broken down into manageable parts. New ideas can be adapted from old one.
4. People think differently in problem-solving situations. Using a logical, patterned approach is often useful. One approach found to be useful includes these steps:
   a. Define the problem
   b. Establish objectives
   c. Get the facts
   d. Weigh and decide
   e. Take action
   f. Evaluate action

F. Training for Results
1. Participants respond best when they feel training is important to them.
2. The supervisor has responsibility for the training and development of those who report to him.
3. When training is delegated to others, great care must be exercised to insure the trainer has knowledge, aptitude, and interest for his work as a trainer.
4. Training (learning) of some type goes on continually. The most successful supervisor makes certain the learning contributes in a productive manner to operational goals.
5. New employees are particularly susceptible to training. Older employees facing new job situations require specific training, as well as having need for development and growth opportunities.
6. Training needs require continuous monitoring.
7. The training officer of an agency is a professional with a responsibility to assist supervisors in solving training problems.

8. Many of the self-development steps important to the supervisor's own growth are equally important to the development of peers and subordinates. Knowledge of these is important when the supervisor consults with others on development and growth opportunities.

G. Health, Safety, and Accident Prevention
1. Management-minded supervisors take appropriate measures to assist employees in maintaining health and in assuring safe practices in the work environment.
2. Effective safety training and practices help to avoid injury and accidents.
3. Safety should be a management goal. All infractions of safety which are observed should be corrected without exception.
4. Employees' safety attitude, training and instruction, provision of safe tools and equipment, supervision, and leadership are considered highly important factors which contribute to safety and which can be influenced directly by supervisors.
5. When accidents do occur, they should be investigated promptly for very important reasons, including the fact that information which is gained can be used to prevent accidents in the future.

H. Equal Employment Opportunity
1. The supervisor should endeavor to treat all employees fairly, without regard to religion, race, sex, or national origin.
2. Groups tend to reflect the attitude of the leader. Prejudice can be detected even in very subtle form. Supervisors must strive to create a feeling of mutual respect and confidence in every employee.
3. Complete utilization of all human resources is a national goal. Equitable consideration should be accorded women in the work force, minority-group members, the physically and mentally handicapped, and the older employee. The important question is: "Who can do the job?"
4. Training opportunities, recognition for performance, overtime assignments, promotional opportunities, and all other personnel actions are to be handled on an equitable basis.

I. Improving Communications
1. Communications is achieving understanding between the sender and the receiver of a message. It also means sharing information—the creation of understanding.
2. Communication is basic to all human activity. Words are means of conveying meanings; however, real meanings are in people.
3. There are very practical differences in the effectiveness of one-way, impersonal, and two-way communications. Words spoken face-to-face are better understood. Telephone conversations are effective, but lack the rapport of person-to-person exchanges. The whole person communicates.
4. Cooperation and communication in an organization go hand in hand. When there is a mutual respect between people, spelling out rules and procedures for communicating is unnecessary.
5. There are several barriers to effective communications. These include failure to listen with respect and understanding, lack of skill in feedback, and misinterpreting the meanings of words used by the speaker. It is also common

practice to listen to what we want to hear, and tune out things we do not want to hear.
6. Communication is management's chief problem. The supervisor should accept the challenge to communicate more effectively and to improve interagency and intra-agency communications.
7. The supervisor may often plan for and conduct meetings. The planning phase is critical and may determine the success or the failure of a meeting.
8. Speaking before groups usually requires extra effort. Stage fright may never disappear completely, but it can be controlled.

J. Self-Development
1. Every employee is responsible for his own self-development.
2. Toastmaster and toastmistress clubs offer opportunities to improve skills in oral communications.
3. Planning for one's own self-development is of vital importance. Supervisors know their own strengths and limitations better than anyone else.
4. Many opportunities are open to aid the supervisor in his developmental efforts, including job assignments; training opportunities, both governmental and non-governmental—to include universities and professional conferences and seminars.
5. Programmed instruction offers a means of studying at one's own rate.
6. Where difficulties may arise from a supervisor's being away from his work for training, he may participate in televised home study or correspondence courses to meet his self-development needs.

K. Teaching and Training
1. The Teaching Process
Teaching is encouraging and guiding the learning activities of students toward established goals. In most cases this process consists of five steps: preparation, presentation, summarization, evaluation, and application.

   a. Preparation
   Preparation is two-fold in nature; that of the supervisor and the employee. Preparation by the supervisor is absolutely essential to success. He must know what, when, where, how, and whom he will teach. Some of the factors that should be considered are:
   1) The objectives
   2) The materials needed
   3) The methods to be used
   4) Employee participation
   5) Employee interest
   6) Training aids
   7) Evaluation
   8) Summarization

   Employee preparation consists in preparing the employee to receive the material. Probably the most important single factor in the preparation of the employee is arousing and maintaining his interest. He must know the objectives of the training, why he is there, how the material can be used, and its importance to him.

b. Presentation
   In presentation, have a carefully designed plan and follow it. The plan should be accurate and complete, yet flexible enough to meet situations as they arise. The method of presentation will be determined by the particular situation and objectives.

c. Summary
   A summary should be made at the end of every training unit and program. In addition, there may be internal summaries depending on the nature of the material being taught. The important thing is that the trainee must always be able to understand how each part of the new material relates to the whole.

d. Application
   The supervisor must arrange work so the employee will be given a chance to apply new knowledge or skills while the material is still clear in his mind and interest is high. The trainee does not really know whether he has learned the material until he has been given a chance to apply it. If the material is not applied, it loses most of its value.

e. Evaluation
   The purpose of all training is to promote learning. To determine whether the training has been a success or failure, the supervisor must evaluate this learning.
   In the broadest sense, evaluation includes all the devices, methods, skills, and techniques used by the supervisor to keep himself and the employees informed as to their progress toward the objectives they are pursuing. The extent to which the employee has mastered the knowledge, skills, and abilities, or changed his attitudes, as determined by the program objectives, is the extent to which instruction has succeeded or failed.
   Evaluation should not be confined to the end of the lesson, day, or program but should be used continuously. We shall note later the way this relates to the rest of the teaching process.

2. Teaching Methods
   A teaching method is a pattern of identifiable student and instructor activity used in presenting training material.
   All supervisors are faced with the problem of deciding which method should be used at a given time.

   a. Lecture
      The lecture is direct oral presentation of material by the supervisor. The present trend is to place less emphasis on the trainer's activity and more on that of the trainee.

   b. Discussion
      Teaching by discussion or conference involves using questions and other techniques to arouse interest and focus attention upon certain areas, and by doing so creating a learning situation. This can be one of the most

valuable methods because it gives the employees an opportunity to express their ideas and pool their knowledge.

c. Demonstration
The demonstration is used to teach how something works or how to do something. It can be used to show a principle or what the results of a series of actions will be. A well-staged demonstration is particularly effective because it shows proper methods of performance in a realistic manner.

d. Performance
Performance is one of the most fundamental of all learning techniques or teaching methods. The trainee may be able to tell how a specific operation should be performed but he cannot be sure he knows how to perform the operation until he has done so.
As with all methods, there are certain advantages and disadvantages to each method.

e. Which Method to Use
Moreover, there are other methods and techniques of teaching. It is difficult to use any method without other methods entering into it. In any learning situation, a combination of methods is usually more effective than any one method alone.

Finally, evaluation must be integrated into the other aspects of the teaching-learning process.

It must be used in the motivation of the trainees; it must be used to assist in developing understanding during the training; and it must be related to employee application of the results of training.

This is distinctly the role of the supervisor.

www.ingramcontent.com/pod-product-compliance
Lightning Source LLC
Chambersburg PA
CBHW081823300426
44116CB00014B/2478